ADVENTURES OF A TERRIBLY GREEDY GIRL

Kay Plunkett-Hogge

ADVENTURES OF A TERRIBLY GREEDY GIRL

Mitchell Beazley

An Hachette UK Company
www.hachette.co.uk

First published in Great Britain in 2017 by Mitchell Beazley, a division of
Octopus Publishing Group Ltd
Carmelite House, 50 Victoria Embankment
London EC4Y 0DZ
www.octopusbooks.co.uk

Distributed in the US by
Hachette Book Group
1290 Avenue of the Americas
4th and 5th Floors
New York, NY 10020

Distributed in Canada by
Canadian Manda Group
664 Annette St.
Toronto, Ontario, Canada M6S 2C8

ISBN 978 1 78472 192 3
A CIP catalogue record for this book is available from the British Library.
Printed and bound in China
10 9 8 7 6 5 4 3 2 1

Publisher: Alison Starling
Senior Editor: Alex Stetter
Art Director: Juliette Norsworthy
Designer: Jeremy Tilston
Copy Editors: Caroline Taggart, Annie Lee (recipes)
Illustrations: Amber Badger
Senior Production Controller: Allison Gonsalves

Dedication

To Mum, and Gran. And Joan, and Sue and Kim
and Claudia. To Joyce, Alice and Corinna and
Ann Marie. To Nora Ephron and Carrie Fisher
and Anita Loos and Mollie Panter-Downes.
To Martha and Julia and Jane and Elizabeth.
To Penelope and Jose and April. To Clare B, Jo,
Jen, Bumble, Paola and Felicity. To Karen, to
Gladys, to Paula, to Alex. To Diana and Heather
and Deb and Julia and Fi and Melanie. To
Adelaide and Veronica and Babs and Lauren.
To all the amazing women who have inspired
me, made me laugh, showed me how a real broad
does things. This one's for you. Cheers gals.

Contents

The Timeline of a Terribly Greedy Girl

The stories in this book are, I suppose, in some semblance of a chronological order. Be that as it may, I am a little fuzzy with dates, so I thought we should probably nail some of them down.

1 9 6 4 ⤳→ 1 9 7 5 ⤳→ 1 9 8 1 – 8 2 ⤳

1964 — Kay is born in Bangkok. Confusingly, her parents were expecting a boy.

1975 — Kay is packed off to boarding school and proves to be terribly uninterested in lacrosse. And cross-country running.

1981–82 — Kay studies fashion journalism at the London College of Fashion.

1 9 8 8 ⤳→ 1 9 9 1 ⤳→ 1 9 9 2 ⤳

1988 — Kay starts working as a booker at Models 1 in London.

1991 — Kay moves to LA with just $500 to her name. Unwise...

1992 — Kay works as the production coordinator on a film called N*atural Causes* out in Thailand. No one has seen it.

1 9 9 6 – 9 9 ⤳→ 1 9 9 9 – 2 0 0 2 ⤳→ 2 0 0 2 ⤳

1996–99 — Kay works as a model booker at Wilhelmina in New York.

1999–2002 — Gets a job at the London office of a film finance company.

2002 — Gets married.

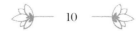

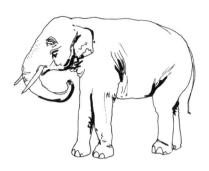

→ 1983 → → 1984 – 86 → → 1986 – 88

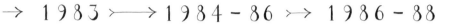

Kay lands her first job: an extra and translator on the set of *The Killing Fields* in Thailand.

Kay attends The Academy of Live and Recorded Arts in London, discovering that she loves radio and is very bad at tap dancing.

While she tries to make it as a singer, Kay works in London fashion stores. She enjoys her staff discount.

→ 1993 → → 1994 → → 1995

Kay goes back to Models 1 in London.

Kay works as a coordinator on *Operation Dumbo Drop*, shooting in Thailand. Not many people have seen this either.

Same job, different movie: *The Quest* with Jean-Claude van Damme. Kay's hand appears in the film briefly.

→ 2003 – 06 → → 2006 → → 2009

Goes back to Models 1. Intermittently. Before heading to Los Angeles for a summer to make her first attempt at writing a book.

Kay starts a catering company and discovers how many bacon sandwiches a lighting technician can eat. It's a lot.

Kay's first cookbook is published.

ADVENTURES OF A TERRIBLY GREEDY GIRL

Foreword
The Omertà of the Dinner Table

When you work as an agent, you learn very quickly to keep people's secrets. You're going to see clients, some of whom will be horridly famous, at their best, at their very worst and at their lowest. Discretion is all. And it's not a habit I plan to break.

Let me put it like this: if you come to my house for dinner, you tell your stories. You may reveal some of your secrets. But you don't necessarily expect those stories or secrets to be repeated outside that context. They are yours. And everyone else around the table should respect that. It is the omertà of the dinner table. A sacred thing involving good food and sealed with some wine spilt on the carpet.

These are my stories. Where required, names have been changed to protect the guilty. People's secrets have been kept. Mine... not so much.

ADVENTURES OF A TERRIBLY GREEDY GIRL

Introduction
Made in Bangkok

I'm gripping tight to my nanny Lune's hand as we push our way through the people-packed market lanes. The air is hazy with smoke. The whiff of grilling pork cuts through the soft scents of jasmine flowers and incense. Mounds of red, green and golden curry pastes loom up from stalls like an edible range of mountains. Flapping fish splash ice and water onto the concrete floors. And there, beyond the piles of fruit, wriggling eels and boxes of fluffy day-old chicks, in a massive wok of bubbling oil, is breakfast: deep-fried savoury doughnuts, ready to be dunked into condensed milk so sweet it will make our teeth tingle. I am six, and this is home.

Is it any wonder I grew up to be A Terribly Greedy Girl?

I never planned to be a cook. In fact, I had set out to be a singer. But, by virtue of Paul Simon's so-called incidents and accidents, I have found myself living a life entirely *un*planned. It has led me from Bangkok to London to America and back. All because, whenever someone has asked me if I'd like to take this job or visit that place, my curiosity has always trumped my good sense. I have found myself cooking in Thai shacks on open-flamed Calor-Gas canisters and high-end ranges in Laurel Canyon homes. I have longed to buy fresh prawns in New York's Chinatown for supper as much as I've delighted in fresh cockles outside Lewisham's Brockley Jack pub with my grandfather.

Even before I ever cooked for a living, food formed the punctuation of my life. As I write these stories and recipes, I realize that this is not a book about how I came to be a cook. It is a book about how I became a woman who *happens* to be a cook. It is about how my Bangkok childhood and living and working on three continents have shaped my take on life and food. It's about how I've tried to learn to take neither of them too seriously. What matters, after all, is not what's in the saucepan, but who you stir it with.

ADVENTURES OF A TERRIBLY GREEDY GIRL

From Lewisham to Bangkok...
with Love

Here's a trigger warning: the following involves coups, spies, GIs, derring-do, the CIA, the Domino Theory, dwarves, go-go bars, drugs and Mum and Dad...

... We open in Bangkok in the very early '70s. The Vietnam War has dragged on for my entire life. Everyone is tired and pissed off. Americans are everywhere; there are rumblings of "Yankee, Go Home!" We've just had a coup, there's another on the way, everyone's seen what's happening across the border in Phnom Phen, Cambodia, and the grown-ups are worried that it might happen here. My father drinks and smokes and sports massive sideburns. My mother uses Nescafé as an upper, and gin and valium as downers. Bangkok's a centre for GI R&R, so the sex trade on Patpong is well and truly roaring. At home, we entertain those very few troops who'd prefer a home-cooked meal to a trawl around the fleshpots. I eat PX doughnuts and get chubbier. We count the B52s in and out of Utapao Airbase, and it seems like a game.

I am eight. I am Jim in *Empire of the Sun* before the Japanese march in. And this is normal.

I still find it hard to grasp the culture shock my parents must have felt when they arrived in Bangkok in 1961. Especially my mother. She and my father had grown up on the same street in Lewisham, south London.

Mum was born in Northern Ireland, the daughter of a drum major in the Yorks and Lancs regiment who'd joined the army at just 15. Dad was a Londoner through and through, born within the sound of Bow Bells, the son of a tannery worker (who, literally, had to taste shit for a living) and a seamstress. They started courting at 13, were engaged at 16 and married at 22, in the course of which Dad endured his National Service, joined the Paras and fought in Suez. And they settled back in Lewisham with every expectation of an ordinary London life.

Except that Dad was driven. (I once mentioned to him that my husband and I were thinking of viewing a couple of houses in Lewisham so we could buy somewhere with more space and he said, "Don't you dare. Your mum and I worked damned hard to get you out of that shit hole.")

People forget that extraordinary social mobility was possible in those

20 years after the war, even despite the ossified British class system. While Mum was the Irish one, Dad was the one who had kissed the Blarney Stone. He took a job in a small south London engineering company, put himself through night school and landed a better job at Ford in Dagenham, where his gift of the gab soon saw him on the sales team, travelling to Big Ford Central in Michigan, then on to Australia and beyond.

I once asked him exactly how he ended up in Thailand. Dad, a man who was full of stories but very rarely stories about himself, was typically reticent, but I pressed the point. It turned out that he had just finished a sales trip to Pakistan and was late leaving the office for the airport, when a call came through: the British ambassador's new Ford had broken down. Was there someone who could fix it? Since it was the weekend, the answer would have been no if Dad hadn't gone and done the work himself. "Well, that's what you did, " he said. At the ambassador's suggestion, Dad was promoted and sent to Thailand as the up-country sales rep for Ford's subsidiary, Anglo-Thai Motors.

He, at least, had seen something of the world. Mum had been to Italy. And Austria. Once.

Still, it was only supposed to be for three years.

Eleven years later, we were all still here.

I still don't know what Mum must have made of the place. My sister Kim was barely one when they arrived. Air-conditioning was a relatively new concept. Hiring staff to work around the house was positively alien, and yet it was expected. And the job took Dad out into the far-flung hinterland of 1960s Thailand, a world where modernity butted hard against a subsistence way of life that had existed almost unchanged for centuries. So, for a lot of those first years, Mum was largely on her own. She never really got to grips with Thailand or the language. She never felt a love for the place like Dad and me. But she made the best of it. Back in London, she had worked as the secretary to a successful novelist (she never told me who; my Uncle George says it was "the bloke who wrote *Brighton Rock*", which has me kicking myself for not questioning her more closely). So here she took a job with the British Council until I turned up in 1964. The year that the Vietnam War broke out in earnest.

It is surreal to live beside a war. For war spills over into civilian life, changing

all it touches. And Vietnam changed Bangkok, and Thailand, deeply. We were on the front line of the Cold War.

In 1954, President Eisenhower, in supporting the French fight against the Viet Minh in Indochina, described the rise of communism in Southeast Asia as akin to falling dominos. If one went down, he argued, the rest would surely follow. So, as the French withdrew from Vietnam, Laos and Cambodia, the US tacitly stepped in (as seen in Graham Greene's *The Quiet American*). Not so tacitly after the Gulf of Tonkin Incident in 1964, in which three North Vietnamese torpedo boats fired on an American destroyer, killing no one. But Robert McNamara, the US Secretary of Defense, subscribed to the Domino Theory completely. And the war was on. Before you knew it, Thailand had US air-force bases, and Bangkok became a nest of spies.

Again, Dad never really talked about it. But on his trips up country, and especially to Khon Kaen, capital of the northeastern region of Isaan, he must have seen what was going on. For this was the heart of the Thai communist movement itself. And, in the years since, I have always wondered what he saw, what he knew, to whom he might have told things over a discreet whisky soda. But he and Mum did their jobs as parents beautifully: Kim and I were never really aware that there was anything to worry about. Even though coups seemed two a penny in the early '70s. After all, when you're a kid coup days are like snow days: there's no school. You don't care if there are tanks on the streets. They're not in your neighbourhood, after all. You get to eat noodles with Lune and to watch cartoons. It's brilliant!

To me, early-'70s Bangkok was a wonderland. GIs gave me doughnuts and Hostess foods – Twinkies, Ding Dongs and Ho Hos – fake cakes with fake cream which, at eight, I thought were marvellous. Restaurants cropped up everywhere to cater to their needs. And Bangkok was shot through with Americana – right down to Dad singing Glen Campbell songs with his guitar – which meant the arrival in town of that perennial favourite of the boys in fatigues, Mexican food.

In later years, I came to regard Mexican restaurants in Thailand as perfectly normal. During the movie-making phase of my career, when we were shooting *Operation Dumbo Drop* in Mae Hong Son, the local Mexican place became

a popular crew hangout. Ten years later, I spent a fruitless evening trying to find an allegedly legendary (try saying that one fast after a few margaritas) Mexican dive in Udon Thani, a journey made in one of the local souped-up tuk-tuks that look like they have half a Harley grafted onto the front, only to find a long strip of girly bars packed with ripped Special Forces dudes. But the Nipa Hut, on Sukhumvit in Bangkok, was the very first. And it was an immediate hit, especially with the ex-pats and especially with me. To the extent that this became my Saturday ritual: spend the morning at the Neilson Hays Library on Surawong, just down the street from Dad's office, then meet him for lunch when he'd finished work (dressed in his Saturday casual working attire, a safari suit with shorts – think Roger Moore in *The Man with the Golden Gun* and chop the trousers off until they're thigh-skimmers) and head off to the Nipa Hut for the Mexican "A" Plate. This consisted of "gringo tacos", refried beans and some kind of rice.

(Before you say anything, foodie types, this was the '70s; this is what we thought real Mexican food was. #Foodie and #Authentic were yet to enter our lexicon.)

To stand out from the crowds, the Nipa Hut's owners thought it would be a novel idea to have a greeter. Rather than hiring a glamorous señorita, as you might expect of a place built to cater to GIs, they decided, a whole decade ahead of schedule, to think outside the box. And signed up a Thai dwarf. They dressed him up in a large sombrero and a little mariachi suit, and he would hop off his stool and run up to open car doors.

I swear to God that, when I first reminisced about this time in my life, I thought I'd dreamed him up, that he must have been some dystopian Lynchian dream I'd had after a particularly bad plate of beans. So I jumped on to Facebook, as we do these days, and, to a fault, all my old pals confirmed the truth. He hadn't been an invisible friend – he was real! And his name was Wee Chai. Online, I even found his photograph. I'm ashamed to admit it, but I was ever so slightly terrified of him. It used to feel like he was chasing me into the restaurant, something I had been perfectly capable of managing on my own for quite a while.

As the '70s ticked on, poor Wee Chai was all I had to be scared of. Along with

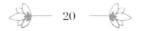

20

snakes and monitor lizards. But Vietnam was spilling over into Cambodia and Laos. And in Bangkok, we had a serious student uprising in 1973, followed by coups in '76 and '77. For the grown-ups, heavy drinking and all-night parties eased the pain – parties I would watch through the bannisters, longing to join in. We could hear tanks rumble up the main road. We could see mortar blasts and fires in the distance. Dad kept guns lined up and ready on the spare-room bed, "just in case". And when the party started to run a little dry, well, Mum would get on the phone to Tom Stores, our local supermarket, and order another case of Johnny Walker. Who cared about the curfew? Not Tom Stores, nor the courier and he'd whizz his moped through the fighting to deliver.

And the party resumed.

But underneath the bonhomie, rumour and skulduggery were rife. Were there Americans in Laos, training the Hmong hill tribes? Yes. Were the CIA based in Bangkok? Yes. Was the person sitting at the next table by the wall some kind of spy? Probably. In fact, there were several definitive hangouts for these nefarious types, and at least one survives. The Madrid Bar, with its carved door and vaguely Spanish interior of wrought iron and checked tablecloths (always the checked tablecloths – why is that?), sat proud in the midst of Patpong. Here, as often as not, you could find characters like Tony Poe, a CIA paramilitary in charge of training the Hmong (he used to pay them to cut the ears off dead enemy soldiers, which he'd nail in bags to the wall at the US Embassy in Vientiane to prove he wasn't making up his body counts), downing beers and talking entrapment. Happy days.

The Madrid is still there, though now it seems rather forlorn, its frontage almost obscured by touts selling ping-pong tricks and sex shows. But once you step inside, the ghosts are there. They seep from the walls. And even if they could, they wouldn't talk.

Saigon fell in April '75. The Laos War ended eight months later. The French and the Americans bailed out and the country closed up; across the border, my parents hid their fears that the next domino, our adopted home, might fall.

21

A Stiff Whisky Soda

....

whisky   **soda water**

ice (optional)

Generally, you'd probably pour a 60ml (2fl oz) double shot into the glass and go from there. But this is a coup. Some bastard's firing tank rounds at a guy who used to be his buddy just a couple of blocks away. And it's a party. So. Go figure.

Pour whisky into a heavy-based tumbler until it's just over half full. Add an ice cube or two, if you're using them. (We're in Bangkok, remember. And it's a coup, so the air-con — hell, the electricity — is not reliable. Use them. Before they melt.) Top up with soda.

If that's not stiff enough for you, repeat. Without the soda. As necessary. Without getting so blotto you can't grab a gun off the spare-room bed if necessary.

They had heard the stories up close – one of the last men out of Vientiane, André Labastie, was a close family friend. He was a handsome, stocky, swarthy Basque Frenchman who couldn't abide English cooking. Brandy butter, he swore, must have been invented to help one swallow the *horreur* of Christmas pudding.

André brought his girlfriend with him. Nittaya, or Nit for short, was tiny and stunningly beautiful, with long, straight, slate-black hair that swung down to her buttocks. She was as hard as nails, but they lived an idyllic existence until she ran off with his driver. Never one to be deterred, André smuggled himself back into Laos and returned with her near-identical sister Nattaya, predictably called Nat for short. She ran off with the gardener. History will repeat itself.

By this time, Kim and I were both at boarding school in England, and the

ADVENTURES OF A TERRIBLY GREEDY GIRL

coups were far away. Except they weren't. They were all over the news. And for the first time, I was terrified. It's hard to imagine now, with mobile phones that allow us to call anyone, anywhere, any time, but in the mid-'70s you still had to book your telephone calls abroad. I remember it all too well, that ghastly, clammy cold at the back of my neck as I sat with my sister in Miss Nixon the headmistress's office, waiting for our call to connect at six in the morning. I remember the relief at hearing Mum's voice, her calm reassurance that everything was fine. But all the calm reassurance in the world is not enough to ease the fears of a 12-year-old's imagination. And even though that coup of '76, which ended three years of shaky democracy, happened far away from our home off the Sukhumvit Road, I don't think I ever quite forgot that creeping feeling that all the things that matter to us – our families, our homes, our cities, our comforts – are as fragile as an egg yolk. They can spill away from us with the slightest puncture, leaving just a stain behind.

You try not to think about it. And so I didn't. Until *The Killing Fields*.

By the time I was 18, I was desperate and determined to be an actress. So when *The Killing Fields* came to Thailand, I had to be a part of it, and I managed to land a job as an extra. My first stint came in a large embassy party scene that never made the final cut (and for which John Malkovich himself fixed a tear in my dress); later, I ran around in the evacuation sequence, in which the helicopters whipped up so much fuller's earth I found it coming out of every orifice for days after. Then they kept me around as a translator. I had no idea about the story. While I chatted with almost everyone, none of it was in any depth – I was more interested in any acting advice they could give me, and most of the cast, especially Bill Paterson, were very generous. When the film came out, we went as a family to see it. I don't remember where. But I remember the deathly quiet as we left. It lasted all the way to the car and beyond, until Dad muttered, "That could have been us."

And that's when it struck home. Eisenhower and McNamara could have been right, and Thailand, my home, my beloved, could have gone. Like Cambodia. Or worse.

I know now that we were lucky.

23

Nit Salad or Salade Vientiane

As the name suggests, this is Nittaya's salad. It's a Laos take on a Salade Niçoise, not spicy, but definitely not French. It became a family staple, made at the beach bungalow in Pattaya, in Gozo on our family holidays and into my folks' retirement. You should note that the dressing is substantial. We always made a lot, all the better to sop up with fresh bread from the local bakery. (You never knew that bread and fish sauce went so well together, did you? Just wait until we get into curry sandwiches.)

SERVES 4 AS A LUNCH

For the salad:

2 Romaine lettuces, trimmed and chopped

2 small endives, broken into leaves

4 spring onions (scallions), chopped

2 eggs, softly boiled

2 × 160g (5oz) tins of tuna in olive oil, drained

For the dressing:

3 garlic cloves, finely chopped

3 tablespoons olive oil

2 tablespoons freshly squeezed lemon juice

2 tablespoons *nam pla* (fish sauce)

plenty of freshly ground black pepper

Mix the dressing ingredients together in a small bowl and leave to stand for as long as you can. Make sure you taste this as you go, to make sure you have the balance right. It should taste salty, lemony, peppery and garlicky, in harmony. People love to dunk their bread in it, so I have been known to double this. And if you don't use it all, it will keep in a jar in the fridge for a few days.

Toss the leaves and chopped onions together in a big salad bowl. Peel and quarter the eggs, and add to the salad with the tuna.

Pour the dressing over the salad and toss together.

Serve with French bread.

 25

FROM LEWISHAM TO BANGKOK...WITH LOVE

ADVENTURES OF A TERRIBLY GREEDY GIRL

And a Turkey in a Palm Tree...

My mother was obsessed with Christmas. I really don't know if this had always been the case, or whether living in the heat of Thailand so far away from home had spurred her on, but she was the original blonde and busty elf – the Dolly Parton of Christmas, if you will. As December came around, Mum came into her own, organizing, decorating, catering. Because Christmas in Bangkok was quite the production.

The decorating took a good two weeks as Mum transformed the house. And by the time it was done, our sideboards heaved with snowscapes made of mountains of fibre-glass wool on which pinecone folk slalomed merrily along past bamboo reindeer. The windows and doors were liberally frosted with snow-in-a-can, and Mum commissioned the Anglo-Thai company artist, Chanin, to recreate her favourite Christmas cards, large-scale to cover the walls.

With the air-conditioning on maximum, and ne'er a glimpse of palm trees outside, we could almost pretend we were living in a Hollywood Christmas and Frank and Bing might pop in for an eggnog at any moment. It may have been 33°C (that's 91°F) in the shade outside, but inside it was Lapland.

Yoon, the cook, worked overtime; an entire shelf of the fridge was taken over, much to my horrified delight, by three curled calves' tongues; a pig was roasted whole; goats were cooked on spits; a towering croquembouche was delivered; and, the Saturday before Christmas, 200 people descended to party.

It is a minor miracle that the house stayed standing. If Uncle Reg (who wasn't really an uncle) had had his way, it wouldn't have. For, in the midst of performing his renowned party piece, which involved lighting a cigarette, dropping his trousers and blowing smoke rings out of his bottom, he inadvertently tapped ash onto the snow scene and sent it up in flames. The elves, tiny pine trees and reindeer: all were ablaze. So was the partitioning wall.

By this point in the evening, most of the guests were so hammered it took them a while to notice. They probably thought it was an indoor fireworks display. But, after a slight pause for the penny to drop, the flames were doused with the soda syphon and about a hundred gins and tonic.

Arson via Uncle Reg's arse notwithstanding, things would calm down a bit before the Big Day itself. Then the Annual Christmas Day Party Marathon began.

27

The day started at five, with bacon sandwiches and cups of tea, followed by a set amount of time to open our presents and tuck them away. Everything bar the gift baskets from Thai friends and colleagues. These had to be displayed so the guests could tacitly show off their generosity later on.

Your average gift basket would consist of some combination of the following: Coffee Mate, Nescafé, Spam, Danish butter biscuits, Plumrose sausages, tinned ham, Chinese preserved plums, Johnny Walker or Chivas Regal. Which left the larder well provisioned until June. At least.

Then, at precisely 8am, we had to be ready to receive two busloads of mechanics and office employees from Anglo-Thai. Food stalls were already set up in the garden to serve *nok kata tort* (deep-fried whole quail), boat noodles, Isaan *som tam* (green papaya salad) and *gai yang* (grilled chicken). Beer, scotch and Coca-Cola were consumed with gusto, cigarettes were handed out like candy, and gambling was actively encouraged. At 11am on the dot, our guests boarded the buses and went on to the next house. Time for a quick freshen up and turnaround before the next group of staff arrived at 1pm until 4pm, for more of the same. But with fewer people. The more senior you were in the company, the later in the day you came. And then, finally, in time for drinks and Christmas dinner, a band of weary ex-pats would trail in to sit, exhausted, and contemplate a full roast-turkey dinner.

The Butterball turkey was imported, frozen, from the States, with a built-in thermometer that popped out of the bird when it was done. This fascinated me. What convenience! What *technology*! And, frankly, after the excess of the day, what a necessity.

With the air-con cranked up to "Arctic", we sat down to dine on pumpkin soup (why, I don't know – can you imagine anything heavier to start a Christmas dinner?), followed by the full turkey works, then Christmas pudding – which I still hate to this day – with lashings of brandy butter. After that everyone staggered into the TV room to watch a repeat of an American Christmas Special and make small talk until they could finally, stuffed and knackered, make their way home.

The only variation to this annual marathon was the year of the Fresh Bird. Chamnong was Dad's Mr Fix-It, a slender Thai man of about Dad's age with

ADVENTURES OF A TERRIBLY GREEDY GIRL

fine, Don Draper-style hair slicked back with Vitalis. I used to call him "snake hips" and wonder how on earth he managed to make sure his perpetually low-slung trousers stayed up. He was the man who could sell coals to Newcastle *and* ice to Eskimos in the same deal, with an added kickback; he could not only find the needle in the proverbial haystack, he probably put it there in the first place. So, when he overheard my mother mention that, one year, it might be nice to have a fresh turkey, just like we would have done "back home", he promised he'd deliver.

You can imagine our excitement.

On Christmas morning, bright and early, before the first wave of staff arrived, Chamnong turned up in a van at the front gate and we all rushed out to greet him. Thrilled by the anticipation in our eyes, he proudly opened the back of his van. And three large turkeys exploded through the doors, gobbling for their lives. The dogs went wild. The cats ran for cover. Feathers and food stalls went flying as, alive and thrilled at a last-ditch chance of freedom, Christmas dinner made a run for it.

I don't know what happened to the turkeys. I did see one of them again, a few days later, roosting in a palm tree next door. And, as for Christmas dinner, well, luckily Mum had been to Tom Stores to buy a Butterball... "just in case".

Duck "Negroni"

Let's face it: when it's just two of you at home for Christmas, a whole turkey is a bit excessive. Which is not to say we haven't done it – Fred has a bit of a thing for a roast turkey – but you do end up with an awful lot of leftovers. (The same goes for goose.)

So when it's just the two of us (and Wilcox, Hepburn and Maya – our cats and the dog have to have a Christmas treat too), I am a big fan of duck. With its crisp golden skin and unctuous flesh, it feels appropriately decadent.

This recipe combines two of my favourite things, a nicely pink roasted duck breast and a Negroni. It's bright and colourful, and with the red of the sauce coupled with the green of some cavolo nero, it looks like Christmas on a plate.

SERVES 2

2 duck breasts

1 shallot, finely chopped

1 garlic clove, finely chopped

125ml (4fl oz) red vermouth

1 teaspoon juniper berries, lightly crushed

the zest of ½ an orange

1 tablespoon finely chopped fresh parsley

1 teaspoon fresh thyme leaves

sea salt and freshly ground black pepper

Preheat the oven to 200°C (400°F), Gas Mark 6.

Lightly score the skin on the duck breasts and season them with salt and pepper. Place a small roasting pan over a medium heat until it's good and hot. Then put in the duck breasts, skin side down. Season the flesh with salt and pepper, and cook for a good 5 minutes or so, until the skin is crisp and golden. Turn the duck, searing the flesh briefly, then put the pan into the oven.

Roast the duck breasts for about 10–12 minutes – by then, they should be nicely pink inside. Remove from the oven and set them aside on a warm plate to rest.

ADVENTURES OF A TERRIBLY GREEDY GIRL

Return the roasting pan to the heat. Pour off all but a tablespoon of the duck fat. Then place the pan over a low heat and add the shallot. Cook the shallot until it's soft and translucent – about 5 minutes – then add the garlic. Cook for a further minute or so, until it's really fragrant, then pour in the vermouth. Add the juniper berries, orange zest and herbs and boil the sauce hard until it's reduced by half. Then strain it through a fine sieve. If it still seems a little thin, pour it into a small saucepan and reduce to your preferred consistency.

To serve, slice the duck breasts on the diagonal. Place them on a spoon or two of creamy polenta. Spoon the sauce around the duck and accompany with some bitter greens or cavolo nero.

AND A TURKEY IN A PALM TREE...

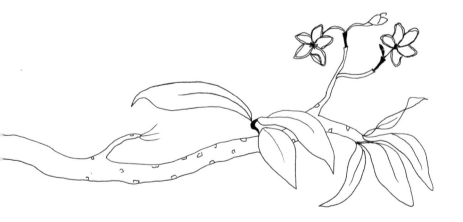

ADVENTURES OF A TERRIBLY GREEDY GIRL

Of Time and the Seaside

When I was a wee slip of a thing, my family would travel down from Bangkok to the coastal town of Hua Hin on Thailand's eastern coast about twice a year. Not so much for the seaside as for the golf tournaments that the grown-ups played in. For us kids, however, it was all about the raw thrill of rickshaw racing!

It was a sight to throw most parents into a fit. Picture three or four children, over-tired, over-Coca-Cola'd and over-excited, each choosing the shiniest, most garishly decorated rickshaw, pressing our baht into the poor riders' hands and racing from the Railway Hotel to the fish market at the end of the pier. As a child – close your eyes – you have the wind in your hair, you taste salt and grilling pork and drying chillies on the breeze. There are no parents. Sand's kicking up into your face, stray dogs are barking, you're laughing till your sides hurt so much you cry. It's heaven.

Back then, Hua Hin was a sleepy town, favoured by families and Thai royalty alike for its long sandy beaches, shallow sea and big Gulf rollers. And, of course, for its incredible seafood. Our favourite restaurant was one of the three based on piers that jut out over the water, a mere skip of a seashell away from the jetty where the fisherman unloaded their catch each day. Chao Lay. Climbing up rickety steps, past tanks of live fish and satiated stray cats, I would feel my excitement mount as I looked forward to picking out my very own *goong mungkorn* (literally "dragon shrimp", a large clawless lobster with long antennae and firm, delicious flesh), cheerfully wresting it away from its chums to its fate inside my tum. Heady days! But days gone by.

The sandy beaches survive, although empty no longer. Quite the contrary: they are packed to bursting with *farang* – foreign – tourists, oiled and seasoned, slowly turning themselves to the colour of freshly sliced tuna, their daybeds packed so closely together that, in order to stroll up portions of the beach, you have to either

a.   Wade up to your knees in water – not great when in a long frock –

or

b.   Walk through the umbrella forest, inhaling the fug of beer, suntan oil,

body odour, cigarettes and garlic, as well as experiencing near darkness in broad daylight.

Today there are girly bars galore. T-shirt stalls seem to be breeding. German alehouses too. Condos stretch from here to Pranburi, some 16 miles to the south, and pretend they're still in Hua Hin.

Progress, they say. Hmm, says I.

But, the restaurants are still there. And so I climb the creaking stairs of Chao Lay and sit down to a plate of chubby-sweet scallops with chillies, lime leaves, basil, green peppercorns and gingery *krachai*... the crispiest garlic squid... a plate of morning glory studded with yellow beans and scud chillies... tiny stripy clams with roasted chilli paste and sweet basil... the ultimate crab curry... and a couple of cold, cold beers while looking out at the King's frigates bobbing on the blue, blue waves. And things look up.

With food like this, some things seem never to change. The sunsets and sunrises are glorious, as if someone has finger-painted streaks of pink and orange sherbet through the sky. There's the kite-seller reflected in narrow strips of water abandoned by the ebbing tide. The dried-squid carts and the ice-cream bikes lit up with neon strips shoot out across the sand. The horses gallop on the damp shore in the cool evening light.

And, at dawn and at dusk, if I squint a little, the beach glows silver and I glimpse the Hua Hin of my childhood.

Ghosts.

The Thais are big on ghosts. They perceive them everywhere. Most houses and businesses have a spirit house, placed auspiciously on the advice of a monk, to take care of them. They're in the rivers, on the roadsides, in the trees. Especially the trees.

Our Hua Hin trips were the exception rather than the rule. Usually we went to Pattaya, where the company rented us a bungalow in a mid-century compound set around a curve of sand and rock we laughingly called Gin Bay. The bungalow was small, just five rooms, plus a covered porch overlooking a low-walled garden with a large frangipani tree, a row of spiky aloe plants and then the sea.

The Thais are superstitious about frangipani. The old name for them,

lantom, sounds uncomfortably close to the word *ratom*, which means "sorrow". Ghosts live in the frangipani. You cannot cut them down, lest you upset the spirit, but they are to be avoided.

That never bothered us. We thought the tree was beautiful. We thought Pattaya was beautiful. Which back then it was – a sleepy fishing town, and the perfect place to escape the city. And, since most of the other bungalows were rented by friends, it often seemed like something of a weekly two-day party.

Dad always worked on a Saturday morning, so Mum, Kim and I would set off ahead of him to open up the house before he arrived sometime after lunch to go fishing. He could stand out there for hours in his swimming trunks and sun hat, fishing for striped bass on the furthest rock from the shore, zinc sunscreen drawn across his nose like a beach-bound Adam Ant until the sun came down and it was time for dinner.

In our absence, the bungalow was cared for by a young man called Preecha. Preecha was not a local boy, but somehow he had settled here and Dad had taken him under his wing. Dad gave him a job and taught him to fish and to drive a boat. And Preecha raised his family here, becoming the caretaker for half the compound.

I think, if he could have, Dad would have happily lived out his days here. But his plan with Mum had always been to return to Europe and, to that end, they had bought a house on Gozo back in 1968. Dad was always one to plan ahead. But he always said to me that it was here, on the Gulf of Siam, that he wanted me to bring his ashes when he died.

I had not been back to Pattaya in years. In fact, I had actively avoided it. In the time that had passed it had become a town of high-rise hotels with added knocking shops. I preferred my memories unsullied. But I had made my promise, and Fred and I drove out of Bangkok with Dad's ashes, and into the past.

It felt as though I was bringing the ghosts with me.

I had feared that the compound would be long gone, but I discovered it still standing, our old bungalow the only one still used and cared for amid its run-down friends. Apart from the 20-storey hotel looming over it, it hadn't changed a bit. I could close my eyes and navigate every room, every nook and

OF TIME AND THE SEASIDE

cranny. I could smell the Saturday curry sandwiches, mixed with the scent of sunscreen. I could hear the screams and splashes as torrential monsoon rain rolled in in sheets from the ocean, the clackety-clack of wooden shutters slammed closed as fans were switched on. The sheer silence when the power went out. It all flooded back in such an urgent throb, it was like a sucker punch to the stomach.

Ghosts.

And there, standing on the terrace with his huge grin, was Preecha, much older now, greyer and slightly stooped, unlike the dark-skinned boy I'd known. His first words were to ask, "How is *Nai* Frank?" It broke me again to tell him Dad was dead. That we had come to scatter his ashes. And that evening, at dusk, just as the sun said its goodbye, so did we, letting the sea take him back to his memories.

And then we went for food. This is Thailand, after all – everything is punctuated by food. While we were here, I had to make my pilgrimage to Na Klua Market where, as a girl, I'd eat warm *khanom krok*, a sort of grilled coconut custard cake, for breakfast while I tried to choose which of the hideously dyed ducklings on sale I could rescue. But I feared the worst. Driving in, we'd seen that Pattaya now resembled Little Odessa without the finesse. I wasn't kidding myself. Pattaya's main strip had always been made up of dives and go-go bars, but this... this was unrecognizable.

And yet, as we entered the village, I saw the old sacred tree still standing and, like the market itself, nothing had changed. It still teemed with fish and prawns, horseshoe crabs and sea urchins, baby squid and blue crab, conch shells and more. And the three families who'd grill your freshly purchased "catch" for just a few baht were still there too, the embers glowing on their barbecues, set beside the pier that jutted out to sea. The skinny street cats still darted to and fro, stealing scraps from beneath the market stalls. The southern Thai girls still sold their pungent curry pastes, redolent with shrimp and chillies, gossiping with their friends and regulars about life, about the boys on their mopeds weaving through the narrow market lanes to deliver Siamese watercress and long beans, coriander and chive flowers, while the men pushed trollies piled with massive slabs of lazily dripping ice from fish stall to fish stall.

We bought too much (how could we not?) and, as we ambled back to the bungalow to cook our rice and dip our fish into the grill man's fiery *nam jim*, I thought once more about the ghosts that we bring with us, the people who are always there, ready to be conjured back to mind through smell and taste, through the sharing of a drink with a mutual friend. Dad loved it here, on this curve of sand and rock. There are still fish out there for him to catch. In my mind's eye, looking out from that ghost-filled frangipani tree, I see him still, standing on a rock, sun hat on, zinc sunscreen spread across his nose, fishing rod in hand, beer at his feet. At one with the world. Maybe tonight I can pretend the fish on my plate is one he caught today.

Khun Nai's Pla Muk Tod Kratiem from Chao Lay

Squid deep-fried with garlic and white pepper

This is one of my favourite dishes on Chao Lay's menu. A couple of years ago, I finally persuaded the owner, Khun Thip, to let me into the kitchen to cook with head chef Khun Nai. I think Khun Thip's secret plan was to teach me the menu so I could teach English-language cooking classes for them. When you think about it, spending three months of the year in Hua Hin is quite appealing. Spending three months of the year in an unair-conditioned kitchen, working with woks on flames as hot as a rocket engine... not quite so much. But I was seriously tempted. If only because I could have this for lunch every day!

SERVES 4-6 AS PART OF A THAI MEAL

2 squid (about 25–30cm/10–12 inches),
    cleaned and cut into rings

3 heaped dessertspoons roughly
    chopped garlic

1 heaped teaspoon stock powder

1½ dessertspoons light soy sauce

1 heaped dessertspoon ground
    white pepper

3 heaped dessertspoons flour

vegetable oil, for deep-frying

Put the squid into a bowl and add the garlic, stock powder, light soy and pepper. Mix lightly but well with your hands. Add the flour, and mix lightly again with your hands.

In a large deep wok, heat enough vegetable oil for deep-frying until hot. You could also use a deep-fat fryer – heat the oil to 190ºC (375ºF). Using your hands, carefully separate the squid pieces and put them into your frying basket or ladle. Lower the squid into the hot fat, then release and deep-fry for about 2 minutes, moving the squid in the fat to make sure it cooks evenly.

Drain on kitchen paper and pat dry.

If you like, serve with some extra deep-fried garlic scattered on top.

Nam Jim Seafood

Thai seafood dipping sauce

I don't know why they don't call this *nam jim talay* but, for some reason *nam jim seafood* has just become a part of the vocabulary. It's fresh, vibrant and delicious.

SERVES 4

6 green bird's-eye chillies, chopped roughly

2 garlic cloves

2–3 coriander (cilantro) roots, chopped roughly

a pinch of sea salt

2–3 tablespoons *nam pla* (fish sauce)

2–3 tablespoons lime juice

sugar, to taste – about 1–2 teaspoons (palm sugar is delicious here, if you have it, but granulated or brown will make a fine alternative)

Pound the chillies, garlic, coriander roots and salt to a paste. Add the *nam pla*, lime juice and sugar. Stir to combine. Taste and adjust to suit your palate: these sauces are not an exact science, so shape it to your taste and around the quality and strength of your ingredients.

Add a splash of water to thin the sauce if needed.

Serve with grilled or fried fish, prawns or squid.

OF TIME AND THE SEASIDE

ADVENTURES OF A TERRIBLY GREEDY GIRL

A Funny Thing Happened
on the Way to the Kitchen

How the hell did I end up here? I ask myself this on a regular basis. I've sold clothes, booked models, insured film finance, coordinated large movies and sung jazz. None of which would lead anyone to think, "Ah, food writing – obviously the next step..."

It was 2002. I had been married less than a year and swore that I was going to have that first year out of work to enjoy the just rewards of waiting until I was 38 to settle down. Then Karen called. Would I come back to Models 1 to look after the older girls? (I'd had a stint there back in the '80s, in the early part of my fashion career, of which more later.)

Every agency I've worked for, and pretty much every agency I know, is broken down into divisions to focus on a specific group of models. There's New Faces, which as you'd expect takes care of the newbies just starting out; there's the Men's division, where I had worked primarily; there's the Main Board – your key girls, the biggest earners. Some agencies might have a Plus-size desk; some might have a Children's division. At Models 1, we had the older girls in a division we called Special Bookings. It represented women who were no longer Main Board but were still in demand, from a few hand-picked celebrities we took care of for commercials and endorsements all the way to the ever-youthful Daphne Selfe and Carmen Dell'Orefice, both well into their seventies at the time and still fabulous (the older I get, the more I want to channel Carmen...).

Now, I hadn't booked a model since 1999. I wasn't sure I could take it. But, being a soft touch, in I went. In six months I had put the division into profit and I had had enough. I felt as if all my energy was being sucked out of me, leaving me feeling like a flat tyre. My long-absent anxiety kicked in – the sort of horror that makes you go over and over and over a document time and again. That made me get off the night bus and head back to the agency to double, triple check the work that had been done that day. I was losing myself down a rabbit hole of my own making. In 1999, when I came back from New York, I had made a decision not to do this job ever again. And here I was. It was time to leave for good.

The final straw was when a certain supermodel called me at home at an ungodly hour of the morning because she didn't feel like going out on the

lucrative job I'd booked her for that day. I had had enough. I was *done*. I went into the agency, cleared out my desk, skipped out again and never looked back. No regrets, not a one. When something is done, it's done.

But. Now I was jobless and married to a writer. Oops.

What to do?

I played around with the ridiculous notion of aromatherapy remedies. But that was far too hippie-dippie for me. Then I thought about vintage furniture restoration, even getting to the point of looking to move TO THE COUNTRYSIDE... forgetting oh so briefly that I have dreadful hand-eye coordination *and* a city girl's wariness of wide-open spaces. And then I was asked to cook for a friend's fiftieth.

Chris was a fashion photographer and an old friend – his wife Zoe and I had worked together in my first stint at Models 1. And he liked Thai food. So Zoe asked me for a recommendation – who could cater his party? "Um..." I said, "I could." Me and my big mouth...

Strangely, cooking Thai food for 60 people felt very much like cooking for a party with my Mum. I felt right at home. Chris loved the food so much, he asked if I could cater a fashion shoot. And my new, totally unexpected business was born. Over the next few years, I catered shoots for *GQ, Glamour, Marie Claire,* French *Vogue,* Danone (which included my brief attempt at food styling: yogurt suspended on a teaspoon – never again), Stella McCartney and more. I loved it. It was fashion – with added calories! It allowed me to dip my toes in the water I loved, yet not have to swim with the sharks.

I never did boxed lunches. I cooked fresh, on location. And if the location didn't have a kitchen, we'd rent a Belling from Rayner's in Wandsworth, and all would be well.

Provisional Menu

Ellen von Unwerth Shoot for River Island
22 and 23 June 2011

DAY 1 – location van
Breakfast
A continental breakfast, including croissants with jams and honey; yoghurt, fresh fruit and home-made muesli; coffee and tea.

Lunch Option A
- A full mezze platter, including olives, pickles, houmous, zhug, labneh, harissa, feta, herbs, crudités and flatbreads
- Imam bayildi
- Chicken, olive and preserved lemon tagine (please advise if you need a vegetarian option)
- Herbed couscous
- Lentil and fennel salad
- Green salad
- A selection of baklava and Turkish delight
- Coffee

Lunch Option B
- Raw, fresh Vietnamese spring rolls with a spicy peanut dip
- Thai southern yellow curry with chicken and pumpkin (please advise if you need a vegetarian option)
- Steamed jasmine rice
- Cucumber pickle
- Roasted aubergine sweet and sour salad
- Bamboo shoot and green bean salad
- Mango and sticky rice
- Coffee

Tea
A rosemary loaf cake with apple snow

DAY 2 – indoor kitchen
Breakfast
A continental breakfast, including croissants with jams and honey; yoghurt, fresh fruit and home-made muesli; coffee and tea. If you would like to add some smoked salmon and scrambled eggs, and we have the kitchen facilities, we can easily oblige.

Lunch Option A
- A mixed mezze platter
- Roasted or steamed Aleppo chicken
- Lebanese yakhnie (a mixed vegetable ragout)
- Herbed couscous
- Orange, radish and fennel salad
- Green salad
- Rosewater and cardamom shortbread with berries and cream
- Coffee

Lunch Option B
- Radish and pea-shoot salad with feta cheese
- Seared, rare English beef with rocket and parmesan
- Salsa verde
- New potato and mixed herb salad with a piquant vinaigrette
- Tomato, marjoram and basil salad
- Raspberry and almond tart
- Coffee

Tea
An orange and almond cake with orange-blossom yoghurt

If anyone thinks catering fashion shoots seems oxymoronic, people do eat on them. Male models, for example, are just regular ravenous young men. Photographers, stylists, VTR units, designers, editors, hair and make-up, the manicure lady – all eat. And, contrary to popular belief, most of the girls eat too. Sometimes I'd have a shoot with an actress who was on a particular diet for a part, especially if it was for a superhero movie, so I'd work that into the menu with her nutritionist or trainer. And it was easy to spot if someone had an eating problem by the constant bathroom breaks. Then I'd gently have a chat to the producer in charge and we would handle it sensitively from there.

I actually miss these shoots now. But I don't know if, these days, my feet and legs could take it any more (one of the reasons I would HATE to be a line cook). And the clean-up – ugh! Especially for one particular client who insisted on white linen tablecloths and silver cutlery...

It was a dinner party that got me an agent. I was up to my usual – chopping, cooking, making bad jokes and asking Fred to mix me a martini – when one of the guests, a friend of a friend, said, "Have you ever thought about doing any telly?" The idea had never occurred to me. But, at her instigation, we shot a little demo and she dragged me in to meet her boss, a TV agent at A Very Big Agency, who took me on and entirely failed to get me a job. Not that I blame her. There is a certain aspect to the job of throwing spaghetti at the wall and seeing if anything sticks. But, though I wasn't sticky enough for telly, it did lead to the following:

```
INT. CIRCA VINTAGE FASHION SHOP - DAY


I'm browsing the rails, touching up the fabrics and
wondering if a spell in traction might make me tall
enough to fit into a really rather gorgeous early-
'60s piece by Dior when —
— my mobile RINGS

                    LOVELY LITERARY AGENT
                  (on phone)
              Kay?
```

                    ME
Yes…

          LOVELY LITERARY AGENT
You write recipes, right?

                    ME
Yes…

          LOVELY LITERARY AGENT
And you know about calories?

                    ME
Yes…

          LOVELY LITERARY AGENT
I need a hundred calorie-controlled
    recipes –

                    ME
Okay…

          LOVELY LITERARY AGENT
– in two weeks.

                    ME
Sure!

Me and my big mouth.

The job was *Cook Yourself Thin: Quick and Easy*. Suddenly I was a food writer. With a literary agent. Which was odd. And rather wonderful. Yet another unexpected twist in this mad thing called life. And I was happy as a clam. Which makes me think... I haven't had clams casino in a while...

ADVENTURES OF A TERRIBLY GREEDY GIRL

A Tale of Two Kitchens

I can trace my cooking roots to two kitchens: my Irish grandmother Sally's, and Yoon's kitchen at the house in Bangkok.

Sally, Gran, was an Ulster woman through and through. Small, tough and uncompromising. Not the warmest woman, if I'm honest, and she gave my grandfather a pretty rough ride. But she was good to me. She probably met more of my school friends than my parents ever did, so she knew me pretty well. And she could cook. Hers was that basic, steadying British cookery that didn't wear any bells or whistles, but comforted and satisfied in equal measure.

She and Grandad lived in a pea-green house on Chudleigh Road in Brockley, and it was to theirs that I would go on weekends out from school or at half-term – all those short breaks when Bangkok was simply too far away. I loved it. Grandad always had a stash of sweets about his person, and would take me frequently to the wondrous Horniman's Museum, detouring on the way home for saveloys, mushy peas and chips ("Don't tell your Gran..."). And Gran would serve up delicious food in epic quantities.

Here we had huge Sunday lunches, with all the family, when we were over from Bangkok. Gran's topside of beef and crusty roast potatoes remain unrivalled to this day. She always served two desserts on a Sunday – a trifle with milk jelly, and a pie. She always had a bowl of stewed apple, spiked with cloves, lurking in the fridge. She'd make cheese scones, which she served warm and dripping with butter. She kept dandelion and burdock in big gallon containers under the sink, alongside bottles of Camp coffee. She made cheese and pickle sandwiches before bed, gave me rock cakes in old biscuit tins to take back to school, and ran the house on tea. Endless cups of tea. All of it served from her kitchen with its wartime utility cabinets, painted pale buttermilk. And all of it cooked on an old New World cooker in the corner, the one with the eye-level grill. There was a door that opened onto the garden path to the outside loo, a serving hatch into the dining room, and a framed print of the Tretchikoff painting *Chinese Girl* on the wall – bought, of course, at Boots in the 1950s. It was a room that hadn't changed that much since Mum and Dad were courting.

Yoon's domain was the "outside" kitchen. It had polished concrete floors, shiny white-tiled counters with three charcoal-fuelled burners along one side with the coal stored underneath. It was a kitchen of bright, dancing flames,

bowls of finely chopped chillies and garlic, filled with the smell of steaming jasmine rice and fish sauce and the sound of lots of chatter. There was a free-standing wooden cupboard with a chicken-mesh front full of salt, spices, tins of Crisco shortening and sun-dried mackerel. Metal stools dotted the large space; a dog or two lounged on the floor, glad to be out of the sun. This was my happy place. I spent far too much of my childhood in there, getting rounder by the minute, but always tasting, stirring, helping and tasting again.

Yoon could cook anything. Literally anything. She had worked for Danish, American and Chinese ex-pats before she came to work for us and, between arguing with my mother over her household budget and how many helpers she could have, she cooked an unprecedented array of delicious dishes, from full smorgasbord spreads and gravadlax to rijstafel, Cantonese feasts, shepherd's pies, American-style towering coconut cakes, chocolate brownies, crab soufflés, roasts of every sort and, of course, spectacular Thai food.

She was a tall woman with short, cropped hair who, in later years, would walk with a pronounced limp caused by a bad fall in which she tried to save my mother's tea set from crashing to the floor. Her leg was properly set and cast, but a soothsayer told her that he could heal it only if she took the cast off. He then magically "produced" nails and screws out of her knee. Suffice to say, her leg healed, but not in the shape of any human leg seen before. She listed to and fro like a ship in a rough sea, which marked an end to her soup-serving days. But. She could still cook.

Both Gran and Yoon relied heavily on fresh produce, bought not from the supermarket but from the green or wet market. And I loved to go with both of them to their respective favourites.

Gran's was Lewisham Market in southeast London. With its loud stallholders and piles of vegetables and fruit, there was bargaining to be done. From here we'd come home with Bramley apples for stewing, rhubarb for turning into jam and pie, pears to poach in cider, King Edward potatoes to roast (that's stuck – I only use King Edwards for roasting and baking), swede to be boiled and mashed with more butter than you could imagine, parsnips to be made into cakes, broad beans to be shelled and popped into your mouth raw as a snack, the remainder steamed, peeled and served with scrambled eggs.

ADVENTURES OF A TERRIBLY GREEDY GIRL

Always fish on Friday. Sardines or herrings rolled in oats and gently fried in butter. Any decent white fillets, dusted with flour and cooked over a gentle heat until sizzling and golden. There was the Saturday treat: going up to the Brockley Jack pub with Gran and Grandad to buy cockles, whelks, mussels, jellied eels and pints of tiny pink cooked prawns. Then home to the daffodil-yellow breakfast room, where we would spread newspaper over the table, grab the bottle of Sarson's vinegar and some white pepper, and greedily tuck in.

In Bangkok, Yoon went to the Asok wet market. Dark and cool under the awnings, it was a cacophony of smells and sights and sounds. Here you'd find piles of galangal and lemon grass, tied into bundles, to be made into *tom yum* soup; garlic and chillies of every hue – staples, of course; mounds of different curry pastes, shrimp paste, roasted chilli paste to be blended into curries and soups; pickled eels to make dips; dried squid to grill and eat, smoky and crisp with a sweet sauce; pork belly to be cubed and blanched, seasoned and fried until it was crunchier than crunchy; beef to be made into *gaeng neua*; fish to be wrapped in banana leaves, roasted over the charcoal fire and served with a fiery *nam jim* seafood. Then there were the snacks. The perennial Thai snacks. *Khanom krok*: tiny grilled coconut custards served in newspaper; *khanom chun*: cubes of brightly coloured jelly flavoured with coconut, jasmine and pandanus; *roti* from the Indian lady, smothered in sweetened condensed milk and rolled up to be eaten hot out of wax paper.

I didn't know it at the time, but all the while I was storing information – these tastes, these smells – honing what would become the palate of my memory. Neither Gran nor Yoon taught me specifically to cook. But in helping them, peeling potatoes or pounding garlic, I was learning by osmosis two very different styles of food. From Gran, I learned that very British focus on simplicity – a great ingredient is a great ingredient, you don't need to mess it about. From Yoon, I learned about *rot chart* – the "right taste", in which everything is about balance between salt, sour, heat and sweetness, from an individual dish to the structure of a meal itself.

Two women, worlds apart. But they shaped how I think about food, how I appreciate produce and how I cook (and how I bargain). I salute them.

A TALE OF TWO KITCHENS

Gran's Stewed Apple Crumble

Gran's stewed apple was redolent with cloves, the smell of which always transports me back to that old kitchen in Chudleigh Road. Leave out the cloves, if you prefer.

For the apples:

6 Bramley (cooking) apples, peeled, cored and cut into large chunks

150g (5½oz) caster (superfine) sugar

6 cloves

For the crumble:

225g (8oz) plain (all-purpose) flour

160g (5¾oz) unsalted butter, cold from the fridge, diced

100g (3½oz) demerara sugar

a pinch of sea salt

Put the apple chunks into a pan with the sugar and the cloves. Place over a low heat, cover and let bubble gently until soft – could be 20–30 minutes. You want a little texture still.

Remove from the pan and pop into a bowl to cool completely. At this stage you can just put it into the fridge and use as stewed apple – serve with porridge for breakfast, with some cream or ice cream or with a slice of rosemary cake – heaven.

If you want to proceed to the crumble, then as the apple is cooling make your crumble mix.

Rub together the flour and butter until they resemble very coarse breadcrumbs. Stir in the demerara sugar and the salt. If you have time, pop the topping into the fridge or freezer for a bit – you'll get an even crumblier crumble.

Preheat the oven to 200°C (400°F), Gas Mark 6.

Place the apples into a lightly greased dish. Cover with the crumble mix and place in the oven for 35–40 minutes, until golden brown and crisp.

Serve with cream, custard or both.

A TALE OF TWO KITCHENS

Yoon's Classic Beef Curry

Gaeng Neua Naa Yoon

This is not a classic red curry – it's not a classic anything, I don't think – but it's the beef curry Yoon would make at least two Saturdays a month and which, the next day, I would sandwich, cold, between two slices of slightly sweet, stodgy Thai white bread to eat, juices dripping down my chin, on the beach. Everyone else did the normal thing and heated it up to eat with rice. Both ways are entirely acceptable.

SERVES 6

For the paste:

10–15 long dried red chillies

2 teaspoons shrimp paste

a pinch of sea salt

1 teaspoon coriander seeds, toasted

1 teaspoon cumin seeds, toasted

2 teaspoons white peppercorns

4 tablespoons chopped galangal

4 tablespoons chopped lemon grass

6 garlic cloves, chopped

4 Thai shallots or 2 small regular shallots, chopped

4 teaspoons kaffir lime zest or regular lime zest

1 large fresh red chilli, chopped

2 tablespoons coriander (cilantro) root, chopped

For the curry:

1 × 400ml (14fl oz) tin of coconut milk

1 tablespoon *nam pla* (fish sauce)

1½ teaspoons sugar

400g (14oz) sirloin or rump steak, cut into smallish pieces

100g (3½oz) pea aubergines (Thai pea eggplants)

4–6 lime leaves, slivered

a handful of sweet basil

Toast the dried chillies in a dry pan or wok over a low heat until just crisp – a few seconds. Remove and set aside.

Wrap the shrimp paste in some foil and place in the same dry pan over a low heat. Roast for about 1–2 minutes, turning once. Remove and set aside.

Chop the dried chillies into small pieces – I use scissors for this.

Pound all the paste ingredients except the shrimp paste together. Remember, the hardest ones go in first. I like to use a pestle and mortar for this, but a mini chopper is also really handy. You will need to add a little water if using the machine. Try to get the paste as smooth as you can. Then stir in the shrimp paste until it is all amalgamated.

Heat some oil in a deep pan and fry 1 heaped tablespoon of the paste until you can really smell it. Pour in half a tin of coconut milk and bring to the boil, stirring until all the paste has been dissolved. Mix until smooth. Add 200ml (7fl oz) of water and the rest of the coconut milk, then add the rest of the paste, together with the *nam pla* and the sugar. Once again, mix until smooth. Measure out another 200ml (7fl oz) of water and add gradually. Use half and then taste. Add the rest if it still seems too thick. You want a loose gravy.

Bring to the boil and add the beef. Bring back to the simmer for 5–10 minutes, or until the beef is cooked through. Taste, and adjust the seasoning – you may find you need a bit more *nam pla* or a bit more sugar, or both. Add the aubergines and the shredded lime leaves, and simmer for about 5 minutes. Then, just when it's ready to serve, taste again, adjust the seasoning if needed, and add the basil leaves. Serve with freshly cooked jasmine rice and some *nam pla prik* (see recipe on the next page) on the side.

Serve hot with rice. Or cold in a sandwich.

Nam Pla Prik

This is the quintessential Thai condiment, found on every table up and down the country.

SERVES 4–6

5 tablespoons *nam pla* (fish sauce)
10 bird's-eye chillies, sliced

1 garlic clove, finely sliced (optional)

Pour the *nam pla* into a small serving bowl. Add the chillies and garlic, if you're using it. Stir it all together, and serve with everything.

A TALE OF TWO KITCHENS

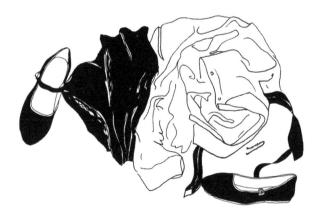

ADVENTURES OF A TERRIBLY GREEDY GIRL

Girls Will Be Girls

A mist-shrouded manor house rises out of a pine forest; some horses malinger in a damp, muddy field; a church steeple pierces the clouds. Bedgebury Park, ancient seat of the influential Culpepper family, who entertained Queen Elizabeth I here in 1573; in my youth a minor public school for girls (oh, how those ghosts must have wept): my first glimpse of what would be my home from home for the next six years didn't fill me with what you'd call an immediate rush of happy.

For a start, it was cold.

And I had to wear shoes.

Had we lived in England, I would never have been sent to a private school. My folks weren't rich, not by a long chalk. But, back then, there were not a lot of options, after the age of 11, for a European education in Bangkok. The magnificent Bangkok Pattana School had done a wonderful job up to that point; from there, it was the US curriculum at the International School or public school "back home".

In those days, as a part of the ex-pat package, the company paid for it – the airfares back and forth, the school fees, everything. If someone's prepared to give your children many thousand pounds' worth of education, I think you'd do exactly what Mum and Dad did, and take the deal. So, in just one generation, my dad went from the Old Kent Road, within the sound of Bow Bells, to having two privately educated daughters who spoke with what were perceived as posh accents.

As it turned out, I had a ball at Bedgebury, even it we did all call it Bedge-itz. I don't remember once feeling homesick. I missed my family and the animals. But I loved school. It was an adventure! I was the kid at Don Muang Airport who was upset if her flight BACK to school was delayed. It wasn't that I didn't have a great time on holiday, it was that I wanted to get back to see my friends.

I didn't care that the fifth-floor rooms had porthole windows with gaps so wide you had to stuff them with paper to keep the cold out, radiators that occasionally coughed into brief periods of action, and beds whose horsehair mattresses bore the imprint of a thousand adolescent girls before me and were the enemy of sleep.

And I didn't care that, being properly unsporty, I was a huge disappointment

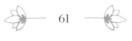

61

to the school. They assumed (never assume, as I would learn later) that the second Plunkett girl to arrive at their doors would be as athletic as the first. Kim played tennis, captained the lacrosse team, swam and was generally an all-round perfect student. She even became Head Girl. I fenced, did drama and sang. I got thrown out of art and sewing for being hopeless. And I refused to swim in the lake – what a vile idea. All that weed wrapping around your legs as though some creature with long, tickly fingers was lurking beneath that green, greasy water, just waiting to drag you down. It still gives me shivers to think about it…

Bedgebury was a very international school. In my first-year class alone, we had girls from Hong Kong, Nigeria, Kenya, the States, Russia, Ghana, India, the Bahamas, Trinidad and, of course, the UK. And by the time we reached the sixth form, we found ourselves all packed together in something of an annex (they called it a wing, but that is far too grand a term), a series of rooms with a common room and, best of all, a kitchen.

Thank God, because the school's food was horrid. Abominable. In my first week, I was told that we would be having curry for lunch. I was blindly excited. Curry! And rice! Like home! I raced to find a good place at the table. I fidgeted all through the compulsory saying of grace. All my little mind could think of was curry-curry-curry…

And then it arrived. It sat in a watery pool of Uncle Ben's quick-cook rice, a grey-brown morass with deeper brown chunks. I poked at it with my fork. Surely that had been a mistake. I took a tentative bite and recoiled. The bits were raisins. Humiliated grapes. And the rest was greasy minced beef over which someone may or may not have waved a spoon of musty old curry powder.

That first curry was a dagger to my poor Anglo-Thai heart.

Salad was not much better, a sad British affair that I soon learned had no relevance to anything I'd ever seen that bore the name: a limp leaf of floppy round lettuce; half an anaemic tomato; an egg boiled to within an inch of its life, halved, bearing the black ring of death around its shrivelled yolk. If we were especially lucky, this excuse for a salad might be enlivened by a slice or two of pickled beetroot. And a large splodge of salad cream would be found squatting at the edge of the plate, threatening all the other participants with its viscous toxicity.

(Dear God, but WHO invented salad cream? And sandwich spread, aka cat

ADVENTURES OF A TERRIBLY GREEDY GIRL

sick? Whoever it was should be banished to the deepest circle of some culinary hell to be chained alongside the demon who thought up Vanilla Coke. *And these damnable things are still available!* WHY?! And chefs – young chefs – are poncing about making home-made homages to this shit. Again: WHY?! It turns out, according to the Internet, that you can polish a turd after all. But the fact remains: it's still a turd…)

Where was I?

School food.

Our favourite tea-time treats were what we lovingly called sticky willies – much to Matron's chagrin. They were those long, slightly sweet buns with a thick streak of sticky white icing. They were delicious. And I don't think we realized quite what we'd named them after… at least not until the fifth form.

After all these horrors, it will come as no surprise that we cherished our sixth-form access to a kitchen. At last, we could COOK. And, a couple of times a month, we did, making dishes from our various countries. There was Yinka's peanut chicken from Nigeria, and Sam's creamy gorgonzola pasta from Italy. I made Thai dishes. The Indian girls made parathas and chapattis by hand, and curries and dahls that put the rest of us to shame. Delphine provided champagne, smuggled in from her family's vineyards. And rumour had it that one of the girls managed to keep her boyfriend in a wardrobe on and off for most of a term.

The opposite sex were a subject of huge interest. Dates were in short supply back home after Dad pulled a gun on one of Kim's beaus and threatened to use it if he didn't bring her home in the same state in which he took her out. At Bedgebury, we had regular dances with the local boys' schools. But these were disappointing. I was never really a fan of all those sweaty mitts and raging hormones that you could smell a mile off. Not to mention the excessive quantities of Brut and Old Spice. Very uncool. And anyway, I was saving myself for Mr Darcy from TV's *Pride and Prejudice*. Or David Rintoul, as he was back then. Before he became Colin Firth.

I even invited him to our final-year party, themed for the Roaring Twenties. What a fine flapper he would find me to be.

He never came.

63

Pad Krapow Moo

Pork stir-fried with holy basil

I think a version of this dish has appeared in every book I've ever written. I make no apology – I'm always refining it. It is my ultimate Thai comfort food, and the most popular Thai thing I'd make when it was my turn on school cooking night. It's hot and fragrant, and was a delicious reminder of home.

SERVES 2 AS A SINGLE DISH, AND 4 AS A PART OF A LARGER MEAL

- 4–6 bird's-eye chillies
- 1 large chilli, cut into chunks
- 6 garlic cloves, peeled
- a pinch of sea salt
- 2 tablespoons dark soy sauce
- 2 tablespoons light soy sauce
- 2 tablespoons water
- a pinch of sugar
- 2 tablespoons vegetable oil
- 300g (10½oz) pork, minced by hand
- 100g (3½oz) green beans, topped, tailed and cut into 1cm (½ inch) pieces
- a large handful of picked *bai krapow*, or holy basil leaves – the more the merrier

In a pestle and mortar, pound the all the chillies, garlic and salt together into a rough paste, then set aside.

Now mix the soy sauces and water together in a small bowl, and stir in the sugar.

Heat the oil in a wok until it's really hot. Throw in the chilli-garlic paste and stir-fry for a few seconds – until you can really smell everything in the pan, but not long enough to colour the garlic. Now add the pork and stir-fry until it's cooked through. Add the green beans.

Now add the liquid and stir through, allowing it to bubble up before adding nearly all the basil and wilting it into the dish.

Serve over steamed jasmine rice, with the remaining basil leaves scattered on top.

ADVENTURES OF A TERRIBLY GREEDY GIRL

For that extra Thai touch, heat about 2cm (¾ inch) depth of vegetable oil in another wok and, when it's super-hot, crack in an egg. Fry until the white is crispy on the outside, and the yolk runny within – it should take about a minute. Drain, and serve on top of your *pad krapow* and rice.

GIRLS WILL BE GIRLS

ADVENTURES OF A TERRIBLY GREEDY GIRL

"It's ALL Fusion, Stupid!"

Food in the '90s was all about fusion. Chefs crashed flavours together, trying to be innovative, putting tastes and aromas that had no earthly business on a plate together, and much of it was disastrous. Worse, they went on holiday to Thailand, and began smothering sticky chilli jam about the place with no clue what they were doing because a) they weren't Peter Gordon and b) they were chasing a fad.

Now it's all swung the other way. Now it's all about authenticity, as if every cuisine on the face of the globe has an incorruptible soul that we must never change.

This, too, is bullshit.

Why? Because with food, if I may steal from James Carville, *it's ALL fusion, stupid!*

Seldom is there such a thing as an original recipe. No one knows who invented the apple pie or the sausage roll or even the green curry. So unless you are a Heston Blumenthal or a Ferran Adrià, the likelihood is that you picked up the idea or the recipe from a meal, an article, a smell, a memory, you brought it home and you played with it.

This is why I never understand why certain food writers are so precious about their recipes. It's six to five and pick 'em that they didn't invent fried chicken or avocado on toast. (Actually, on the subject of the latter... I think I *might* lay claim to that one – in the '80s, yes *the '80s*, when I worked at Models 1, I used to have the café across the road make me a toasted bagel with Marmite, avocado, tomato and basil... so there!)

None of the chefs I've ever worked with are precious about recipes, though they are exact about them. They realize that their recipes are fusions and evolutions. They learn them from each other, from each kitchen they move through, passing combinations and techniques from chef to sous chef to chef de partie, from kitchen to kitchen. They refine as they go. They evolve. They fuse things together. And they know where, by and large, they came from.

It's the same with your family. Your gran taught your mum, who tweaked it a bit; then she taught you, and you tweaked it too. Perhaps you didn't like the mushrooms in it, or fancied more rosemary.

Every recipe therefore tells a story, because food, at its heart, is not about

ingredients (though obviously they're important). It is really about people.

This is why I learned to cook in the first place: to spend time with interesting people. And one of the things about people is that some people travel. They travel for trade, they travel for war and they take things with them.

I have always wanted to follow that mad brooding general Alexander the Great on a food journey to the East. From Macedonia, he rages through Turkey, the great cities of the Levant, conquers Persia and Egypt, goes native, pushes almost to China through Afghanistan, comes back through the Punjab and dies in Babylon. All the way he travels with a massive army, on foot and on horseback. And what travels with armies? Whores and cooks. So what came first: feta or paneer?

The roots of food fusion, where cultures collide and create something new, go back this far and further. They are key to civilization. I just have to look to Thailand, with a food culture that seems so singularly unique, to see how the influence of Indian, Chinese and Persian merchants shaped its cuisine, arriving in-country and adding coconut milk and cream and local ingredients to spice mixes of their own. *Khao mok gai* is nothing more than a Thai version of a biryani. *Gaeng heng lay* is a curry built on a meeting of Burma and China in the heart of the old Thai kingdom of Lanna. The Thais in turn start pounding these ingredients into pastes with pepper, their preferred spicing ingredient until, at some point in the early 16th century, the Portuguese turn up. With chillies. Which come from Mexico. How is this not fusion?

We don't have to look into the dim and distant past to see this kind of organic, unpremeditated fusion in action. We just have to hop on a flight to Los Angeles. America has described itself as a melting pot since 1908. Taking this literally, the roots of dishes like Philadelphia pepperpot, a tripe-based dish that is clearly a variation on a Caribbean pepperpot, said to have been created through expediency during the Siege of Valley Forge during the War of Independence, go back to the earliest idea of an independent United States. In LA, as the revered food critic Jonathan Gold put it, you can on a night out find not just a new dish but an entirely new cuisine. Why? Because different ethnicities live side by side. And they connect in the first instance through food, as their kids come back from school and run in and out of each other's houses. Is there a

more powerful engine for food change than Junior saying, "Mum, can you make this like Mrs Miggins down the road?"

This is how true food fusion, not the artificial '90s version, happens. And it has always happened. Since the things we need to live are food, shelter and safety, it follows that these are the first things we talk about when we meet new people. That's why, as food writers, we need to tell the stories of the origins of the food we love. It reveals new truths, reminds us of old wrongs that, by eating together, we can mend. It tells us why food matters. Honestly, I don't give a fuck about a good marrow. I give a fuck about my neighbour. If I can prepare that good marrow in a way that makes them happy, I have put something good into the world.

Sashimi with Thai Salsa Verde and Dill

This is a glorious example of the new fusion in Thai food. I could have gone for something Thai-Talian, a mash-up that's hugely popular. But this Japanese-Thai melding is so zingy and exciting, I cannot resist.

When you make this, make sure your salmon is spankingly fresh sushi-grade fish. Tell your fishmonger what you're up to. And don't make the sauce too far ahead – this whole dish relies on being made as close to eating as possible.

SERVES 4 AS A STARTER

For the dipping sauce:

a large bunch of coriander (cilantro), leaves only, chopped finely

3 garlic cloves, chopped

2 tablespoons *nam pla* (fish sauce)

3½–4 tablespoons lime juice

1 teaspoon sugar

4 green bird's-eye chillies, chopped

2 coriander (cilantro) roots

For the fish:

250g (9oz) raw salmon, sliced thinly

3–4 garlic cloves, sliced paper thin – 1 slice per slice of salmon

some fresh dill (Lao coriander) – enough to put a sprig on each slice of salmon

First make the dipping sauce: place all the ingredients in a blender (I use a small herb chopper – the blades are just the right size) and whizz until fairly smooth. Pop into a dish and set aside covered with cling film (plastic wrap).

Place the salmon slices on a platter and top each slice with a thin slice of garlic and a small sprig of fresh dill.

Serve immediately, with the sauce on the side. You should eat the salmon with a jot of sauce on top of it.

70

"IT'S ALL FUSION, STUPID!"

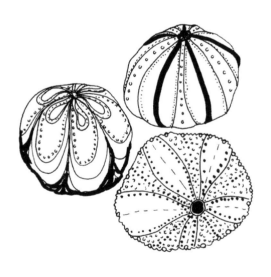

ADVENTURES OF A TERRIBLY GREEDY GIRL

Carry On Sailing...

Ah, *Muscadet*! So many happy days and nights.

For once, we're not talking about wine. *Muscadet* was a yacht, 32 feet of polished teak and 1920s craftsmanship. My father was always determined to learn new things. So, after he retired to Gozo and before he decided to become the Zen master of the internet at the age of 75, he set out to learn to sail.

Dad bought *Muscadet* off a salty old dog called Mike Carmichael. He and his wife June were terribly, terribly British. She was fearless. She would hum and whistle even in force 8 gales. He would shout and tell me I was no better than a masthead. And they had sailed her around the Mediterranean and back many times. But now they were getting old, and a wooden boat's hard work. Enter Dad.

From then on, we would take a sailing holiday every summer, a glorious journey that took us first to the majestic Grand Harbour in Malta to clear customs, then across to Sicily, where we would toodle along the coast eating, drinking, laughing.

The first trip especially stays in my mind. We were all still novices, though Dad did know the ropes somewhat thanks to a few lessons with Mike. Still, we thought it would be a good idea if Mike and June came along. So there was our family of four, Mike and June, and our dearest friends, Fleming and Shirley Kinnaird. Fleming was a dark, swarthy Scot with a sly sense of humour and very small trunks; Shirley a tall, auburn, loud, funny Canadian with a penchant for large whiskies and terrible ordering in restaurants.

Provisioned with water, wine, gin, scotch, more gin, more scotch and plenty of Fray Bentos pies, we set off.

The sun shone as we put out from Grand Harbour and into the wild blue yonder, Kim and I in our bikinis (well, Kim in one; I was and am more of a one-piece gal). This would be a doddle.

The first clues that it probably wouldn't be came when the wind started gusting, about three hours into the trip. "Never mind!" shouted Mike. "Just a bit of a breeze, old boy. Let's set the sails and use it!" Then the rain started. We should have known. Storms in the Med come fast out of nowhere. Since we'd put out from Malta, we should've asked St Paul. The wind came up. And up. We were far too far out to turn back now. Mum was crying. Shirley was clutching

a large scotch. Fleming was asleep – for here was a man who could sleep anywhere at any time. June was still whistling and humming. Dad was looking worried. We were all told to go downstairs, pray and batten down the hatches. We would have to ride it out.

It lasted about an hour of constant pitching, rolling, yawing, vomiting and crying. Repeat. Then, as suddenly as it had blown up, it was gone. The sea was like mill water and the skies were blue again. Normal service resumed.

With only a few hours before nightfall, we made dinner – tinned pie, heated up in the little Belling on board. We hit the wine, hit the gin, topped Shirley up with scotch, and drifted off to our very compact sleeping quarters.

I say quarters. They weren't really *any* quarters as such. Just cubby holes that we shoved ourselves in. All of us. Below decks. Very cosy indeed. I couldn't stand it. The snoring. The farting. The constant stream of loo going. Too much, darling. Too much. I headed for the deck, damp or not, and under the stars I slept like a baby, woken only by the distant lights of giant tankers and the low murmur of Dad's radio as he stood watch.

Landfall was the tiny fishing hamlet of Porto Palo. Swim, wash up, dress, put ashore. For our first meal in Sicily.

I wish I could remember the restaurant's name, for I remember the meal well. We ate outdoors on a patio overhung with ripe, pungent lemons, their smell lingering as the heat of the day faded and the cool brine air came whispering in from the sea. They served the freshest seafood – fat swordfish, rich tuna, gleaming anchovies, fire-red shrimp and coral-coloured sea urchins. It was astounding. We don't have swordfish in Thailand; we have marlin. Which is good. But this, seared firm and juicy, bathed in olive oil, garlic and oregano, was revelatory. My first Italian food *in Italy*.

Morning brought strong coffee and fresh fruit. There's nothing like ripe peaches and nectarines eaten on deck, the salt air mingling with their sweet juices, the breeze ruffling hair, espresso in hand.

Siracusa was only a dot away, so off we sailed for this storied city on the sea. We moored behind the main harbour, where the fishing boats did, away from the danger of high winds, something we had learned to do from a dear friend who'd lost his yacht, *Nyata*, a few years before when a storm lifted her onto the

74

dock and smashed her. That, and the personality of the canals, as we called them, was better. As soon as we docked, fishermen bartered fish for cigarettes and beer. I was whistled at and called *bella*. Oh, what bliss for a 14-year-old girl!

That first dinner in Siracusa... We were joined by a younger couple who were friends of friends, and seemingly nice. But then, at the table, I felt a warm hand rise up under my dress. It wasn't Mum, to my left. So it could only be HIM on my right. Calm down, I tell myself. Don't make a fuss. You are in Italy, after all. You've been told such things are "to be expected". (Yes, we were really told things like that.) I didn't know *what* to do. I stood up, excused myself and went to the bathroom. It turned out that that was enough. And when I told my parents, they laughed, so I laughed. And it did seem funny. Then.

Apart from the annual Sicilian trip, *Muscadet* would ferry our family and friends out to Comino and Cominotto, the small islands between Malta and Gozo, where we would while away summer days swimming, drinking copious amounts of wine and diving for sea urchins, which we cracked against the rocks and sucked on with relish. Never one to cut corners, Mum would insist on cooking quiche for the guests on board. Why, I have no idea. I remember many a birthday spent in the Crystal Lagoon when, sunburnt and tired at the end of the day, I'd be allowed to wallow in the tender and be towed home behind the boat, glass of something cold in my hand, the cooling air drying the salt on my skin.

Then it was all off at the harbour and up to Gleneagles – probably my Favourite Bar in the World™ – to wash off the day and enjoy one of Tony's Negronis, watch the horses being exercised in the sea and the fishermen packing up their nets.

We loved that boat. In my mind, she is always associated with great food and good times. Sometimes, we'd even drive down to Mgarr just to picnic on board, sailing into a nowhere of our imaginings. Then came the time when Dad felt like Mike and June: it was becoming too much work. Age catches up, no matter what. *Muscadet* was sold and it was time for pastures new. Still, as the movie says, we'll always have Paris.

CARRY ON SAILING...

Sicilian Swordfish

This simple treatment of the mighty swordfish always brings the Sicilian sunshine flooding back. Make sure you use the freshest oregano you can find, and serve with a cracking Caricante from Mount Etna.

SERVES 2

2 swordfish steaks, just over 1cm (½ inch) thick

For the sauce:

4 tablespoons extra virgin olive oil

1 garlic clove, finely chopped

2 tablespoons sea salt

the juice of ½ a lemon

2 tablespoons chopped fresh oregano (or 1 of oregano, 1 of flat-leaf parsley)

1 tablespoon capers, chopped (optional)

sea salt and freshly ground black pepper

In a small saucepan, gently infuse the olive oil with the garlic over a low heat until fragrant. Do not let the garlic colour. Then set aside to cool.

Dissolve the salt in the lemon juice. Stir in the herbs, then whisk in the olive oil and garlic until emulsified, and season with pepper.

Grill the swordfish steaks over a medium-high heat until cooked, turning once. It should take 5–7 minutes in all. Place them on a serving platter, prick them gently with a fork, and pour over the sauce. Scatter over the capers if using. Serve straight away.

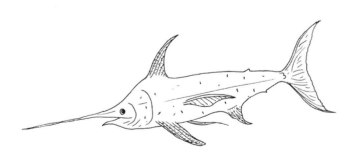

CARRY ON SAILING...

ADVENTURES OF A TERRIBLY GREEDY GIRL

Hollywood or Bust

(or LA Stories)

"Welcome to Hollywood," says a man at the start of *Pretty Woman*. "Everyone comes to Hollywood got a dream... What's your dream?"

This is my dream.

I always wanted long hair. Luscious, thick and glorious. Golden, like caramel, that dipped over one eye. Hair like Veronica Lake. In fact, at the tender age of six I would steal my mother's lipstick, paint my pout scarlet and pretend I was her in *I Married a Witch*.

Alas, it was never to be. My hair was fine and wavy, and tangled easily. Brushing it out was horribly painful, provoking screams from six-year-old me of "*Jep! Jep!*" ("It hurts! It hurts!") as I fought free of Mum. But that early brush with Hollywood glamour made me crave the Celluloid City. Perhaps there – yes, there – dreams could come true.

My first foray to the City of Angels did not start well. I had planned to go with two friends. I had saved a few hundred pounds, and the plan was to jet off to seek fame and fortune. The three of us would share a flat and all would be well.

Except that Jason and Anne decided not to go.

But me? I was all in. I had already jacked in my job and bought my ticket. Staying in London was not an option.

And it got (potentially) worse from there. I landed in LA with nowhere to stay. This is something Customs frowns upon. But I had managed to speak to a friend of a friend, who had a friend, who would help me out. I had never met him; I hadn't seen a photo of him. And he was late.

I was slightly terrified.

The friend was the wonderfully named Sandro Reinhardt, to whom I'd been introduced by Jose, who owned Models 1 (on whom more later), when she decided that he and I should make a promotional film for the agency. Sandro and I made an unlikely pair. He was 6 foot 7 inches; I was 5 foot 1 inch. But we got along famously. So, when Anne and Jason (frankly) welched (sorry, chaps, but you kinda did), Sandro stepped into the breach to volunteer his buddy. Josh.

Nowadays, Josh and I would have probably Skyped before I got there. At the

very least, I would have had his mobile number, even a picture on my smart phone so I could pick him out of a crowd. Instead, this being 1991, I was stuck kerbside at LAX, sporting neither a red carnation nor a copy of the *Daily Telegraph* under my arm.

And then he turned up, a cheery chap with a mop of curls and an easy smile, to find me stranded like a human Paddington, *sans* label reading "Please look after this model agent", and whisked me off to his apartment in Santa Monica, where he lived with his pocket Venus of a girlfriend, Yvette. On the way, we stopped on Ocean Avenue to watch the sun set over the Pacific. I fell in love with LA right then.

It always struck me as rather magical that my two favourite cities, the ones where I felt most at home – the one where I was born and the one in which I hope to end my days – are both called the City of Angels. Both are mad sprawls of concrete and steel, freeways and skyways. Both are loved and loathed in equal measure. Both, on closer inspection, reveal themselves to be a maze of interconnected villages, each with its own character. But, while one is a jewel of the East, the other is a metaphor for the West.

America was built on the myth of the West, that place beyond the horizon where you could carve a new life from the wilds. In Los Angeles, there is no more West to find; it is curtailed by the ocean. So instead you come here to carve your own West out of dreams. It's no accident that LA is a factory town for two great industries – aviation, building machines to fly into the future; and motion pictures, building hope and story out of flickering lights in the dark. No wonder, then, that Frank Lloyd Wright, an architect famed for building dreams of the future out of concrete, described LA as a town to which, if you picked up America and shook it, all the things that were not nailed down would come.

Thanks to Josh and Yvette, and Josh's sister Gaby, my crash-landing in LA couldn't have been smoother. Before too long, I was renting a room from a friend and ready to chase my dream. And here I learned one of the most valuable lessons of them all: if you're going to a new city, and someone at home tells you they know someone whom you should look up – do it.

Jose (again) told me to call her friend Clare, who had been on the books at Models 1, but had recently started her own business in California, providing

ADVENTURES OF A TERRIBLY GREEDY GIRL

locations and production services to fashion shoots. So I did. And soon found myself sitting at her dinner table next to Barbet Schroeder's ex-girlfriend, who told me that his ex-assistant was preparing a movie shoot in Thailand. Two phone calls later, I had a job. And I learned the second lesson: when people tell you it's not what you know, it's who you know, they're telling you the truth. Especially in a town like Los Angeles, where the default response to your attempt to get a job is generally "Why not?", as opposed to the London version, "Why?" Of course, having talked your way into the opportunity, you must then deliver, because there are rarely second chances.

(The job in question was as a production coordinator on a film called *Natural Causes*, working for Joan Weidman, who became my mentor in film and, after a puppy I had rescued on a Thai beach covered her head to foot in explosive diarrhoea, one of my dearest friends.)

All this is possible because LA *is* a factory town. If you've come out to break into the business, you will rarely be more than two steps from some sort of access. Which is one of the reasons why almost all waiters and waitresses at even slightly upscale restaurants have a script or a résumé hidden under their aprons. It's also how you can find yourself at a party asking Barbra Streisand if she could pass the mustard. (Although, if you really want to know how to get anywhere in Hollywood, you can do no better than to follow Bette Davis's immortal advice, "Take Fountain." Check a map.)

People make a lot of presumptions about LA. Because of the picture business, people decide it must be a very superficial place, full of air-kissing and back-stabbing. If all you've ever seen of it is Beverly Hills or Santa Monica, it's easy to have such a prejudice confirmed. More so if you find yourself queuing in the supermarket behind that not-so-rare creature, the 1880 – someone (alas, generally, a woman) who from behind, in her white leggings (all the better to show off her pert buttocks and perma-tan), looks 18, but looks 80 from the front, where the plastic surgeon's attempts to hide her age have drawn her belly button to where her nose once was. Yes, LA is obsessed by the new. But it does have depth. It has history and culture. Just because that history is shorter than a lot of other cities', it doesn't mean it isn't there. And its obsession with the new means that a history of past new things is drawn upon it.

81

People also assume that a place with so much sunshine must be hiding something sordid in its shadows. LA has its dark side. It is a city of shocking contrasts, with enormous wealth on the one hand and awful, abject poverty on the other – something that should be disgraceful in a state which has, on its own, the eighth largest economy in the world. And, as a city built on dreams, it can be shockingly cruel to those whose dreams sour and who are unable to steer their lives to other goals, or even to goals of their own.

As with all things, all places, there are pros as well as cons. There is Laurel Canyon, cool and green and full of wild cats, deer, dalmatians and old hippies. There are the beaches, though I wouldn't swim off one any nearer to Santa Monica than Point Dume due to the sheer toxicity of the water – every time I see the surfers, I hope their vaccinations are up to date... There's the weather. How could you not love the weather? Except when it rains, which isn't often; then, every Brit watching KTLA's *Storm Watch* thinks, "Stop whining, it's only a shower," and every Angeleno forgets how to drive and the freeways turn into a high-speed game of bumper cars. The cinemas are terrific, with proper big screens, comfy seats and decent popcorn. The produce is incredible – this desert-turned-oasis churns out fruit and veg to die for. The driving can be a drag, but, hell, that's why I have a husband.

It makes me think – in the 19th century, they presented California as the cornucopia of the West; after the war, they sold LA as a city of opportunity – in my experience, there is truth in advertising.

And Hollywood? As the man in *Pretty Woman* says, it's the Land of Dreams: "Some come true, some don't. But keep on dreamin'."

HOLLYWOOD OR BUST

My Ivy on the Shore Salad

The sun is shining, the sea breeze wafts up from the shore, I'm seated at my favourite shady table on the terrace, chilled glass of rosé in hand, warm molasses bread on the table and an Ivy Grilled Vegetable Salad with Shrimp is on its way.

I'm in LA.

Except, all too often, I'm in my kitchen in London on a grey and drizzly day. One bite of this, though, and I'm transported back again...

SERVES 4

500g (1lb 2oz) raw tiger prawns (shrimp), peeled and cleaned

2 tablespoons vegetable oil

1 teaspoon Cajun spice seasoning

2–3 courgettes (zucchini), quartered lengthways

1 bunch of asparagus, trimmed

6 spring onions (scallions)

2 ears of sweetcorn on the cob

2 heads of Romaine lettuce, chopped

2 avocados, peeled, de-stoned and diced

2 large tomatoes, deseeded and chopped

1 lemon, quartered, for serving

For the dressing:

1 tablespoon freshly squeezed Meyer lemon juice (or fresh lemon juice mixed with a little fresh orange juice)

3 tablespoons olive oil

Cajun spice seasoning, to taste

sea salt and freshly ground black pepper

You will also need some bamboo skewers soaked in a bowl of water and a barbecue or a cast-iron griddle pan.

Fire up the barbecue or a griddle pan to a medium heat. Drain and dry the skewers.

Thread the prawns on to the skewers, ready for grilling, and brush with 1 tablespoon of the vegetable oil seasoned with the Cajun spice.

84

Toss the courgettes, asparagus, spring onions and corn in the remaining vegetable oil.

Now for the grilling. The corn will take about 15 minutes, the courgettes and prawns about 7 minutes, the spring onions and asparagus about 5 minutes, depending on their size. So put them on to the heat accordingly. Keep an eye on everything, turning them so that the corn ends up with slightly blackened bits all over, the other vegetables have nice char-lines and the prawns are pink, flecked with spices, and cooked through.

Meanwhile, place the chopped lettuce, avocados and tomatoes in a bowl.

Mix together the dressing ingredients.

When the prawns and long vegetables are done, remove them from the heat and take the prawns off their skewers. Chop the long vegetables into 1½cm (½–¾ inch) chunks, and cut the corn off the cob with a sharp knife. If you like, and depending on their size, you can chop the prawns to the same size too, but they're fine left whole.

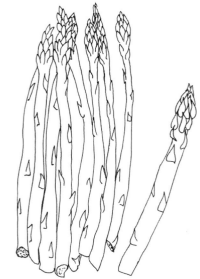

Add the prawns and vegetables to the salad. Toss all the ingredients together with the dressing, and serve at once, with lemon quarters.

HOLLYWOOD OR BUST

10 Flying Dos and Don'ts

Okay. Some of these are food tips, some of them are etiquette. After all, as Jean-Paul Sartre says, hell is other people, a line I think he must have conceived on a 12-hour flight in economy. So here are my tips to make your long-haul flight a little easier:

1. Create your zone. This is just common sense. I always travel with a small bottle of lavender oil with which I douse my travel pillow. This should be enough to ward off most unpleasant odours. If not, you may have to ask to be reseated...

2. Long haul or short haul, ALWAYS bring a bottle of Tabasco. It's under 100 millilitres, so you're allowed. And it will make even the foulest airline food moderately palatable. Let's face it, at 30,000 feet, our senses of taste and smell are seriously diminished – not even Heston Blumenthal can do much about that – and that's before we factor in the kerb appeal of our little plastic tray. This is food that needs all the help it can get. And, as an added plus, you'll have it to hand for your Bloody Mary – the best sky-high drink, allowing you to rehydrate as you dehydrate. So now you can make yours as stonkingly hot as you want.

3. Who ARE those people who pull themselves up with the back of your seat when they get up to move around? Could they not use the arm rest? Or their own sense of balance? They're almost as bad as the ones who lean on your seat back while they loiter in the aisle to chat to someone seated nearby. There should be a special circle of hell reserved for people who fuck unnecessarily with the backs of other people's seats, and it involves being kicked in the back by a small child in perpetuity. Unless they are very old or infirm. Then we are to be kind to them. Actually, while we're on the subject of the backs of seats, let's also glance quickly to the sides: the feet sticking through the gap in between the seats in front of you, whether they be be-socked or not... it's just horrific. I have a very sensitive nose (as do many). These people should keep their feet in their zone; then we'll keep our glares in ours.

4.   Bring your own food, especially if you're flying economy. Carrots, an apple
     or two, a small bag of nuts and dried fruit – that roughage is vital, and your
     bowels will thank you on arrival. On which point, avoid cold sausages of
     any type. They will stay with you well into your holiday. If you don't have
     time to prepare anything, the Nando's in Gatwick's South Terminal is a
     godsend. Eating peri peri chicken at altitude is one of life's great pleasures.
     Similarly, if you're flying out of LAX, swing by Canter's for a takeaway
     sandwich. I favour the roast beef with extra mustard. I now have them
     briefed to put the pickle (that would come on the side) into a lidded soup
     pot to avoid leakage. And I've been tempted, out of Bangkok, to swing by
     Soi Polo Chicken, but I fear this might be a step too far. Because
     excessively smelly food is a crime against your fellow passengers. On
     which point: never bring a durian on board. Or even contemplate eating
     some in the 24 hours before boarding.

5.   Make the stewards and stewardesses your best friends. It's a sign of very
     low character to be rude to waiters in restaurants, doubly so at altitude.
     Bear in mind that they only get paid when the aeroplane doors are closed,
     so they could've worked a 13-hour day and only been paid for five. These
     poor men and women are tired and their feet hurt. And they're here for
     your safety. Everyone deserves courtesy; these guys deserve a standing
     ovation.

6.   The toilets. Oh boy! Where do I start? Beyond our little zones, we're in
     a negotiated space on a flight for anywhere from one to 17½ hours, and
     nowhere is this more evident than in the toilets. For the love of all that's
     good in the world, you'd think some people could wipe off the seat! And,
     if they're male, just pop it back down. This isn't some latrine in the damn
     forest. It isn't hard. And it has a flush on it. None of us want to be
     confronted by a lake of someone else's wee at the best of times. So I
     propose that Her Majesty gives a medal to whomever invents a device that
     ensures you can't unlock the toilet door until the loo's been flushed. That'll
     teach 'em!

10 FLYING DOS AND DON'TS

7. When the seatbelt sign is on and they ask us to return to or remain in our seats with our seat belt fastened... I wish-I wish-I wish that people would actually DO IT. They aren't saying it for fun. First up, the crew have to tell the cockpit about this illicit scamper to the bathroom, which means that, if the plane's coming into land, the loo-bound party can delay the entire plane. And, in turbulence, they could be thrown across the cabin. We've all seen footage from the zero-gravity-simulating "vomit comets". What goes up must come down so, all for the sake of grabbing something from the overhead locker, little Mr I Know Best might fall on me. Or you. Or someone you care about. I worry about this *a lot*.

8. While we're on the subject of safety – why doesn't everyone watch the safety film?? I've tried to tot up the number of hours I have spent in the air. It's in the multiple thousands – and I always watch. Even if they are Little Miss Experienced Flyer, who's been on every kind of aircraft known to man, every carrier does it slightly differently, and we're all in it together when the shit comes down. So if I see someone reading a book, or chilling out to some music, believe me, *if* the time comes that we ditch in the sea or crash in the Andes, they are on their own, buddy. We will be sliding down that inflatable ramp, clutching our heels, without them.

9. Bless all those that have children. And for travelling with them. I think it's terrific. But please, if you're not prepared to render them insensible with Calpol (it worked for my mother), then at least keep the little buggers under control. I don't see the amusement in little Camilla's kicking my seat back. One game of peekaboo with Lily is quite enough – I am not the in-flight entertainment. And if little Tarquin gets his pecker out, it's really not that funny. Also, would you please change diapers in the toilets (see point 6). Thank you.

10. I am more than happy to chat, especially for a little while and especially on a short-haul flight. I think we all probably feel the same. But please, when I politely pick up my magazine, smile and turn to my husband, or put on a movie... that means we're done. It's the sort of thing that makes you grateful that they now serve our dinners with plastic cutlery....

10 FLYING DOS AND DON'TS

ADVENTURES OF A TERRIBLY GREEDY GIRL

Dumbo, Drug Lords and Spies in the Mist

Starring an imported elephant, Disney and (allegedly) the DEA

It wasn't the most auspicious start to a new job. I was accused of being a traitor, of siding with the *farang*. All because I took a job with the Yanks.

The movie was called *Operation Dumbo Drop*. Shot in Thailand and based – very loosely – on a true story of an elephant that was parachuted into a village during the Vietnam War, it had a great cast, a good director, an irritating little boy in a lead role, a sorry script (I didn't see the draft that was green-lit) and confused marketing. It was not a success.

But I digress.

From the title and the premise, you will gather (obviously) that an elephant was involved. Several elephants, really, but one of them was a MOVIE STAR elephant. Tai was a gentle young ingénue of 26 when she joined the picture, as yet unaffected by fame and a career that would see her go on to work with Brendan Fraser, Eddie Murphy, Banksy and Bill Murray. She was flown in from her home in sunny California, on Korean Air, handled by FedEx. I still have the manifest somewhere – cargo: 1 elephant; weight 8,000 pounds. She had to drink and be bathed in bottled water, and had her special feed flown in from the States. And she wasn't supposed to fraternize with local elephants. So perhaps it wasn't wise of us to start a rumour that she had become intimate, shall we say, with a Thai bull elephant and was with child. We even mocked up documents. Poor Steven the production manager went apoplectic. What was he going to tell the studio? How soon would she start to show? What about the insurance? Hell, could we find another elephant? We had to come clean. Eventually.

In our defence, it was a bloody long shoot. I've heard it said that Denis Leary claims it was one of the worst experiences of his life. I don't remember him being too miserable. Perhaps it was because he couldn't get a tuna sandwich when he wanted one. Poor Denis.

But I remember it as being rather wonderful. I mean, what's not to love: being

91

in northern Thailand in the winter; having elephants all around you; eating Thai food every day; making lasting friendships; singing endless rounds of bad karaoke; buying ophthalmology equipment for a rural hospital; saving a baby elephant? Come on! What kind of party pooper wouldn't enjoy that? Let's weigh the scales: on the one hand, we have *yum neua*, *larb khua* and a great curry; on the other, a tuna sandwich. I know which one I'm picking, and I think Willem Dafoe (whom Denis sometimes pretends was in the film instead of him) would agree with me...

It was an adventure. Yes, there was the small issue of Khun Sa, the infamous Shan warlord and self-confessed Opium King, who wasn't *too* happy with us playing war games in his 'hood. Yes, he *may* have shot at one of our helicopters one day. On purpose. And yes, there was a kidnap threat or two, especially against poor Tai. All in a day's work, I say. And he did invite our favourite producer, the lovely, late Penelope Foster and me to tea up at his fortress. Via one of the crew, who turned out to be a Shan lieutenant. Just keeping an eye on us. Letting us know all the best places to eat... But Disney wouldn't let us go. Pshaw! Spoilsports.

I suspect that this was because of a persistent rumour – and, for telling this, I will probably be banned from Disneyland forever – that our crew had been infiltrated by DEA officers disguised as Vietnamese extras. I can't say who I heard this from, not just because they'd probably have to kill me, but also because I can't remember. But there were a couple of minor drug busts while we were up there, followed by a major sting and lots of arrests not long after we left. Everyone I mention it to now shakes their head and looks vacant. But if you think about it, what a brilliant idea! Officers, dressed as fake officers, in a movie, arresting officers *in a fake army*.

We shot 1993–94. It can't be entirely coincidental that, after such a long location shoot, they had to finish up against a green screen in Orlando. Nor that the DEA managed to shut down Khun Sa's access to cash and supplies the following year.

Khun Sa "retired" in '96.

Just saying...

I still think it would have been curious to meet him.

But back to the movie. No one talks about the people in the production office. On our shoot, there were four of us, Sue, Michele, Amy and I. We were the ones who made sure that everything made it to where it was supposed to go – actors, crew, equipment (film and military) – we made sure everyone had the right hotel room and access to laundry. We made sure, at the end of every day, that the film cans were correctly labelled (with the camera guys) and that every two days they were put on an internal flight to Bangkok and thence to LA. Still, about once a week, someone would wander into the office and ask one of us, "Are you the fax girl?" Yeah. We're just the ones you complain to when your hair dryer doesn't work. Yes, I do know the number of a good doctor so you can have an AIDS test before you go back to your wife, you fool. And yes, I do happen to know a guy who can fly the director, DP and first AD from Bangkok to location in Mae Hong Son when there are no commercial flights because the airstrip's fogged out.

We were the girls who got shit done. Sue was a feisty, take-no-prisoners Irish American with a heart of gold. She was the one who, when the chips were down, would say, "Look it: this is what needs to happen…" No nonsense, no bullshit, a woman who could (and did) lay her own living-room floor. I loved her at once. Michele was from Seattle, a kooky, grungy rock chick who looked so young she could have been a "band aid" out of *Almost Famous*. Amy had a beautifully maintained beehive and didn't like rice. For that reason alone, I'm not quite sure why she took this gig, and we all wished she would join in more. We were up before everyone else, were mooned by Ray Liotta more than once on his morning jog (not wholly unpleasant – we all loved Khun Ray), were last back to the hotel. We learned how to make the best of things.

We had the ways and means. We had almost adjoining rooms on the third floor, with a great view of the forest. We had regular care packages of salsa, chips and tequila, sent by Erin, our opposite number in LA, and wine shipped in from Bangkok on a weekly basis. When we finally got back to our rooms, after a really long day, it was our bliss to sit on our balconies, listening to cicadas and Tom Jones (TJ's in the house!), and sip a delicious glass of Côtes du Rhône. We held regular picnics – girls only – where we packed up and headed for a nearby waterfall. No actors allowed. Though Ray often tried to crash. (You know you did, Ray.) Then there were the parties – the karaoke nights, with... Thai Elvis. In Thailand, as in many countries, Elvis acts are huge. So when, one day, there was a buzz in downtown Mae Hong Son because the local-boy-made-good Elvis impersonator was coming back to town, we had to go. And we had to make an effort. We dressed in mohair sweaters and headscarves and headed into town for our big night. Lo and behold, not only was he the town's local hero, he was the Thai Elvis from my local restaurant in LA. The hound dog! We sang "Blue Hawaii" and "Rock A Hula Baby" in the jungle, made like Ann-Margret and danced till almost dawn.

It was in Mae Hong Son that I discovered one Thai dish I've never been able to find since. Its name was *moo nork kork* – literally, pigs outside their sty. They made it at a restaurant called the Fern, which I believe is still there (I haven't been up there for such a long time), and I had to have it every time I went. It was pork, deep-fried in a coating that tasted like ground rice and other *larb*-esque spices, crisp and giving, with that savoury umami hit that, once tasted, makes you crave it.

I have searched everywhere for a recipe. I've found only one other restaurant that even knows about it – Pailin in LA's Thai Town. It joins *pla suea*, a dish I had with my dad in a town called Tak, as one of the two dishes I want to find again more than anything.

Even then, I was on a quest to discover and eat the Thai food reserved for locals. Language opened up towns like Mae Hong Son for me, and I was able to bring my friends along for the ride. But I understood too the crew's need for something familiar. It doesn't matter who you are, Thai or *farang*: there comes a point where you want to eat *something else*. Sometimes, after a long stint on the road, you crave a room-service burger. It is unavoidable. On this shoot, in addition to Mae Hong Son's one Mexican restaurant – a leftover from the *Air America* shoot a few years before – our unit favourite was an Italian place in Chiang Mai. The Piccolo Roma. Last time I was there, we swung by for the sake of old times just after service (coming back from my friends' restaurant, Puong Thong, which you should make a point of visiting if you happen to be in town). The chef-owner was in. I introduced myself. And we sat at a table, drinking Ramazotti on ice, reminiscing about the time Danny Glover insisted on making

94

the calamari the way he liked it (excellent, by the way) and other instances of drunken table dancing.

On *Dumbo Drop*, we ranged all over the north and central plains, from Mae Hong Son to Lopburi – Monkey Town. Really. With so many men in army fatigues and guns and planes, it felt like we had gone to war.

And then we were done.

It was time to pack up. One of the younger actors asked me to help. I did. End of. And then I was summoned.

There were drugs in his boxes. And I had packed them.

Now, you've read the papers. You've watched TV. You may even have heard of the "Bangkok Hilton". So you know that, in Thailand, drugs smuggling is a *very* serious thing. Back in the day, like President Obama, I liked a joint. I inhaled. But I wasn't stupid. There's no way on God's green earth that I'd try to take a drug across a border, let alone Thailand's.

"Drugs?" I asked. "What drugs?"

"This!" I was told. And, with a flourish, the saddest, smallest, most lint-covered piece of dried grass I'd ever seen was produced. It had so obviously been in someone's pocket for years. Until five minutes ago.

"And what else was in the box?" I asked.

"Papers." Lots and lots of papers. I knew for a fact this wasn't true – I hadn't packed any papers, just clothes and books – and it felt as though I was being set up for something, some perceived slight. But if this was a prank, it had already gone too far. In retrospect, I was lucky that it was so pathetic. If it had gone any further, I could have been in serious trouble.

And, with the next prank, I was.

Since the shoot had run so long, I had had to take the crew's passports in order to extend their work visas. But two of them – who happened to be in charge of all the weapons on set – decided that, because of this, I was involved in some complicated plot to trap them in Thailand. Why, I don't know.

(Let me interject here: Aussie crew – no moaning, no complaining, great guys. British crew – a bit of moaning (come on, it's a national pastime), but pretty good with any issues like no hot water. American crews – oh, boy! I had to rescue one of them from a spider in the bath, fix the hot water, remove the

naked-monkey carvings from the hotel room, put in cable, go to Bangkok and record 49ers games and transport them back BY HAND.)

(Disclaimer: the author states that this her own experience and is not casting aspersion on all US crews... some of whom are marvellous people and *very brave*.)

Anyhoo.

When we wrapped, these two left Thailand as fast as they possibly could. Buggered off to the good old USA without, as they say, so much as a "by your leave". As well as leaving, they also left their arsenal. Which had to be shipped back, and they had put the shipment in my name. So Amy and I headed to the airport, her with her beehive, me with my pixie cut, to ship arms to the States. We thought nothing of it. Until everything passed through the X-ray and, suddenly, we were surrounded by a lot of men with guns. Shouting.

This is scary.

We were led to a detention room, poor Amy in tears, me on the verge of them, though at least I could understand what was going on, to be questioned for an hour, images of Thai prisons swimming before our eyes. It was only when I reminded them of Tai the Elephant's arrival that they calmed down enough to tell us what was going on.

There was LIVE AMMUNITION in the shipment. It had not been declared. And it was in my name.

It could have been a prank. It could have been an oversight. I could have gone to jail. It was only thanks to the beautiful Tai, and the Thais' reverence for elephants which ensured that they remembered her, that I was able to talk my way out of it.

Thus endeth the lesson.

96

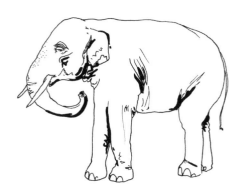

DUMBO, DRUG LORDS AND SPIES IN THE MIST

A Thai "Sai Oua" Burger

Everyone craved burgers on this shoot. So I felt that they should have one, just for them. This is based on a traditional northern Thai *sai oua* sausage, which I have turned into a burger patty. The original recipe comes from the *very* brilliant Vatcharin Bhumichitr's book, *A Taste of Thailand*. For anyone looking for a straightforward Thai cook book – this is it. Vatch is The Man. His recipes are foolproof. And that he isn't as much a superstar as the brilliant Ken Hom is a mystery to me. My copies of his books are literally in pieces from overuse.

MAKES 4 BURGERS

For the burger patty:

750g (1lb 10oz) minced pork

5 coriander (cilantro) roots, finely chopped

12 lime leaves, finely sliced

4 garlic cloves, finely chopped

2–3 sticks of lemon grass, very finely chopped

4 Thai shallots, or 2 regular shallots, finely chopped

2½cm (1 inch) piece of galangal, finely chopped

3 tablespoons good quality red curry paste

3 tablespoons chopped coriander (cilantro) leaves

1 teaspoon dried roasted chilli powder

2 teaspoons turmeric

2 tablespoon *nam pla* (fish sauce)

4 tablespoons cooked rice

To cook:

1 tablespoon vegetable oil

To serve:

4 good brioche-style burger buns

sliced red onion

sliced tomato

sliced cucumber

lettuce leaves

cheese slices (optional)

crushed peanuts

sweet Thai chilli sauce

sriracha mayonnaise (mix 1 part sriracha sauce with 2 parts mayo)

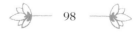

98

Mix all the burger patty ingredients together thoroughly in a large bowl, really mushing them together with your fingers until everything is combined. Set aside for 2 hours, if you can, to let the flavours meld.

Meanwhile – prep your add-ons.

Form the meat into 4 even-sized patties.

Heat a non-stick pan. Rub the patties on both sides with the vegetable oil. Fry until they're cooked through, turning from time to time.

Serve in the buns, with all or any of the add-ons you like, and cold bottles of Thai beer.

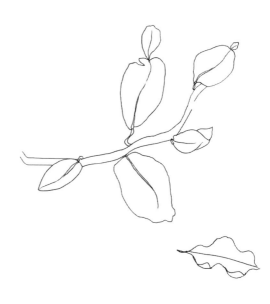

DUMBO, DRUG LORDS AND SPIES IN THE MIST

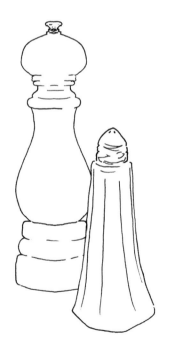

ADVENTURES OF A TERRIBLY GREEDY GIRL

And Another Thing... 1

Dear Restaurants,

Just put the salt and pepper on the bloody table. If I want it, it's not an insult to you or your cooking. I may just want to lightly salt that artisanal butter that you've probably had rolled between a virgin's thighs at some dairy in Albania.

That is all.

Models, Mayhem and Martinis...

Part 1. The Beginning

Once an agent, always an agent. There's not a day goes by that I don't find myself peering over my glasses at some unsuspecting young person, sizing them up before I catch myself and realize I look like a middle-aged pervert. So, sorry if it was one of you... old habits die hard.

I don't know of anyone who ever said, "Ooh... I fancy being a model agent" (or a booker, as we call ourselves – a terrible term which sounds far too much like hooker, and throws up images of one officiously stamping papers in saucy lingerie). But into it I fell, like every other job I've had since my extremely short-lived singing career (another story for another book, folks) shrivelled and died.

In the months that followed, I worked in a variety of fashion stores – Joseph and Kenzo most notably – bored senseless by the standing around, but delighted by the 33 per cent discount. Here I started to mingle with models while I helped out at the shows. I fell in love with the world. And, quite by chance, a model said he thought I would make a good booker. (See – that damned word again: I HOPE he said booker.) So I met with a headhunter and, a week later, found myself at Models 1.

On the Men's division.

My first official duty, so my new boss told me, was to measure all the boys' inside legs, just for the record. Tape measure in hand, I steeled myself to the task, my face turning redder and redder as I was confronted by groin after groin. Behind me, my new colleagues struggled to conceal their mirth. But they'd given me a job, and I was damn well going to do it — you don't grow up with my Dad's sense of humour and not learn how to take a joke. As hazings go, you could do a lot worse. Now I was part of the gang, ready to look many a crotch straight in the eye. Without blinking.

The second order of business was that I had to change my name. Another Karen had started there just weeks before, and they couldn't have two Karens. It would be confusing for the clients. And the models. It had to be something with a "K". I thought of Krystal or Karmen or Kristina. "Oh, for fuck's sake,"

said Karen. "Just call yourself Kay and get on with it."

Jose and April had opened Models 1 in 1968, and ran it still. Jose was slight and beautiful, still a bit of a flower child but with a mind like a steel bear trap. April was so opposite to her that it worked – suits and stockings all the way, the yin to Jose's yang. Dick, who ran the Men's division, was Jose's husband: arch and with a sense of humour so dry it would give a martini a run for its money, he had a penchant for tight jeans and steak tartare, and he was utterly lovable in a strange, masochistic sort of way, damn him. Between them, they laid the foundation for my agenting years. I started on the Men's division, but did sojourns on all of the boards – New Faces, Women, Hair and Make-up. But I always came back to the boys. They were so much easier to deal with. You could shout at them, if need be —

                    ME
           (calling a model at a casting)
         Paul, where's your portfolio?

                    PAUL
         It's right here.

                    ME
         Then why am I on the other line with
         someone who's just found it in a phone box?

                    PAUL
         Er…

– and not have them burst into tears. They weren't as vulnerable, and they were easy on the eye. It was like dealing with a few dozen good-looking little cousins. I loved it.

It was the '80s. The new Summer of Love was about to happen, money was being thrown around like dollars at a stripper, business was great. Models 1 celebrated its twenty-first birthday and the stars came out to play. I wore black

palazzo pants, a black sequined halter-neck top, and experimented for the first time with fake tan on my bare midriff. (I was 23. It was about time.) It turned out that the fake tan didn't like dancing as much as I did. It wanted to go home early. So you can imagine my mortification when I found myself at a table with Joan and Jackie Collins, praying that they wouldn't notice it was dripping from my torso.

They remain the most glamorous women I have ever, ever met. And I have met a few. If they ever tried fake tan, it would damn well behave itself, stay in place and be grateful.

Every Friday, we had drinks in the agency while we wrapped up the week's business. The boys came in and hung out. Cigarettes were *de rigueur*: the ceiling was obscured by an ever-thicker fug of smoke and, by the time we were done, the ashtrays resembled little alps of butts. Davina ran clubs around town, where we partied hard. And once a week we would take over Pucci's on the King's Road along with the rival men's agency Select. Dancing on the tables to the Gypsy Kings and living like there was no tomorrow. Barring an occasional gasoline fight, I was deep in the world of *Zoolander*.

Intermission

Here's a thing. Again. (Perhaps this book should have been called *Rantings of a Terribly Greedy Girl*.) It seriously pisses me off when I hear literary agents or acting agents or, frankly, any other kind of agent sneering at model agents. All right, that word "booker" doesn't do us any favours. I mean, you don't hear of a "book booker" or an "actor booker"… but… if they had even half our workload… (and here I can only attest to agencies I have worked for – reputable and with a great duty of care). A model agent is, in essence, a friend, a therapist, a conduit for work, an accountant, a PR, sometimes a lover (though I stand by the old saying "Don't get high on your own supply"), all things to all models. We worked bloody hard for our talent. If a model was coming into town for the first time or hadn't been to town in a while, we organized go-see after go-see – at least five to eight appointments for them every day – to put them in front of the cream of London fashion. We formed relationships with photographers and clients, so we could push our models, so that they might pop to become the next big thing. And we didn't just book them into any or every job – we strategized their careers, especially in New York, where our thinking was always about the long game. Take... let's call him "Bob". His London agent wanted to book him for Top Man. But we knew that Top Man was right across the street from Donna Karan's office. We knew "Bob" was her kind of boy. But if she saw him in Top Man's window, it was never going to happen. So we nixed it. And he got the Donna Karan, a gig worth four Top Man campaigns or more.

We worked our arses off. In the only industry I can think of where women earn more than men on a consistent basis. So there.

Part 2. The Middle

I was in Milan for Men's Fashion Week in the mid-'90s when I met Laura, a rather lovely English gal who worked for Wilhelmina in New York. We got on famously, drinking wine, swapping stories, laughing at the boys' tales of dancing for dollars (when model work was scarce, the Milan clubs would pay the boys to come and dance, look gorgeous and entice in other punters. It's a living). She suggested I make the move to the Big Leagues. New York City, baby. So I did. I flew out, interviewed for the job, got the job, went home, packed my bags. And that was that: I'd just moved to the City at the Centre of the World, and I'd only ever spent one night there. Some would call me foolish...

New York was a whole different kettle of fish. Those first few weeks, I didn't know what had hit me. Here I was, in a strange city, working in a team that included one or two of the most hard-nosed, arsey people I had ever met – rude, aggressive, bullying, irrational – but this was The Show: I was in the world's most successful men's agency of the time. The boys were beautiful – dizzyingly, distractingly so. The money they made was astonishing. The expense account was glorious. Yes, I was made to cry about twice a week. Yes, I vowed never to turn into some of the vicious bookers I worked with. I stayed three years, so... as the saying goes, work in New York, but not for so long that it makes you hard... and I learned to love a solitary martini at my local bar, Odeon.

To make an extra buck and to get out of NYC, I signed up to scout models via an independent outfit. Loads of us did it. We were paid about $300 a time and flown out to exotic locales like Kansas City, Missouri, or Reston, Virginia. We

ADVENTURES OF A TERRIBLY GREEDY GIRL

A Diet Coke and a Pack of Marlboro Reds

This is the quintessential model's meal. As you will see, it is packed with all the major food groups... that can kill you...

1 can of Diet Coke

1 packet of Marlboro Reds

You will also need a lighter.

First remove the plastic from the cigarette packet. And the inside foil. Remove a cigarette. Only offer to other people if asked. Open the can of Coke. Light the cigarette. Smoke. Drink. Do not even think of having another Coke until you've smoked at least three more cigarettes. Then repeat.

were put up in chain hotels, and fed and watered so long as, bright and early on both Saturday and Sunday mornings, we were preened and ready to meet the hordes of aspiring models.

These hopefuls could be anyone, regardless of size, creed or colour. We looked at 'em all, be they aged nine or 99. The organizer took money from all of them, and sold them posters with life-affirming quotes and books on "how to be a model" – tomes you could boil down to this one sentence: win the gene-pool lottery. Let's face it, most of his punters didn't have a nun's chance in hell of becoming a model. But no one has ever lost money selling people a shot at their dreams. For our part, we were encouraged to jot down a few names, ask questions and ask some of them back for a "sit down". The horror. And to add to the atmosphere, the organizer would play "Eye of the Tiger" before we agents trooped in, taking our seats Simon Cowell style, to pass judgement.

There were all sorts of shenanigans, contestants spied coming out of agents' rooms and all manner of really bad behaviour. I managed about half a dozen of these weekends before I realized I would rather stick a rusty fork in my eye than ever take part again. Bye bye, Miss American Pie. On the upside, however, these trips introduced me to an America I would never otherwise have seen. They took me to New Orleans, where I discovered the glorious restaurant Dooky Chase; I went to Kansas City – great barbecue, line-dancing with cowboys, won the bucking bronco contest on a mechanical bull; Austin, Texas; Santa Fe, New Mexico. I had always loved American food – all those Hostess snacks from the PX in Bangkok – now I was able to see it, in situ, in all its diverse and regional glory.

That said, the food wasn't always all it was cracked up to be. I only went to Cedar Rapids, Iowa, the once. It was the year *everyone* went, properly representing their agencies. The year before, they had discovered a handsome small-town boy who'd go on to be a massive TV star and the third ex-Mr Demi Moore. Ashton Kutcher. He was killing it as a model, so agents came from all over the world, with Ashton himself in tow, to see if we could find another Midwestern Adonis. The hospitality we were met with was charming in the extreme. But there was something of a culture shock as the fashion world was served corn product after bland corn product (it's truly horrifying, the things you can do to corn) and Coca-Cola on tap. Rosa from Milan was all but screaming, "Where's the fucking wine? *Ma Dei!*" I would have killed for gin. And we made it out of there with a lovely boy called Aaron. Very cute. He and his girlfriend eventually headed to LA, and I have no idea what happened after that. If you're out there – give me a call.

Intermission

There's always the One Boy. I mean, we represented dozens, nay, hundreds of these gene-pool lottery winners, but there is always one who everyone falls a little bit in love with. Each agent has a favourite. (Come on... it's like parents who say they love all their kids equally. I call bullshit on that. You love some more than others and in different ways. So it was with models.)

My total unequivocal favourite was the one who, weirdly, everyone kind of crushed on. The one we all agreed on in a game of "Would you or wouldn't you?" I don't think I met an agent or a client, male, female or non-binary, who didn't have a little moist spot for this one. He wasn't classically handsome, but he was striking and so, so stylish. He oozed sex. His name was Gerard Smith. We always wondered if Smith Jerrod in *Sex and the City* was modelled on him...

3. The End

After three years in New York, I was exhausted. I was beginning to get hard around the edges and, even though I had my own guest list at Joe's Public Theater, I was becoming aware that it was time to leave. I had just signed a contract for another two years. But I came into the office on a Tuesday to experience such a shit storm of pettiness and aggressive behaviour that I stormed into the boss's office, plucked my contract from his in box and said, "No more." Then I picked up the phone to Joan and said YES to her offer of a job back in London. I was out.

On one level, it was a big decision. On another, it was the easiest one I've ever made. Ever since I had ended my first stint at Models 1 to go to California, my dual careers in film and fashion had always intertwined. It was time once again to answer the Call of the Celluloid. That said, as soon as my choice was made, I felt an enormous rush of relief. Like the apocryphal frog in the kettle, you

don't notice the heat building up around you when you work under that kind of pressure, day after day – this despite contracting *Erythema nodosum* from the sheer stress of it by the end of my first three months. I walked out onto Park Avenue South and, like Mary Tyler Moore, tossed my proverbial hat in the air – I was going to make it after all, just like her – partying up a storm with friends to celebrate "Thank God We're Not British Day", aka July 4th, before jetting back to Europe.

Do I regret it? Not for a moment. Would I change it? Well, it was a wild ride. But you can't ride wild for ever – you'll get blisters on your bum. Every so often, when I spot some young hottie and that "Yes, we could book you" thought creeps through me, I think of my friends who stayed in – Susie the Super Scout, Karen who's now the boss cat, and the rest – the ones who could walk out of the agency at the end of the day and leave their worries at the office door. I'd had my fun. But, for me, the music had stopped. And it was time to go.

MODELS, MAYHEM AND MARTINIS...

Risotto Milanese

Ah... Milan! One of the things I loved about the Milan shows was the chance to eat this silky, glorious dish in its home town. Ideally in Rosa's company. With wine.

SERVES 4

2 litres (3½ pints) chicken or veal stock

a good pinch of saffron strands, soaked in a shot glass of hot stock

60g (2¼oz) unsalted butter

1 small onion, very finely chopped

30g (1oz) veal or beef bone marrow

400g (14oz) Vialone Nano risotto rice

125ml (4fl oz) dry white wine

20g (¾oz) grated fresh parmesan, plus extra for sprinkling

sea salt, to taste

First bring the stock up to the boil, then turn it down to a gentle simmer and draw off a little to soak your saffron.

In an enamelled cast-iron saucepan or casserole, melt 30g (1oz) of the butter and gently fry the onion and bone marrow until the onion is soft. Add the rice and stir it in well, making sure it is well coated in the onion and bone marrow mixture. Now add the wine, stirring gently until almost all of it has been incorporated into the rice. Now add the saffron and its soaking stock, along with a good ladle of the stock on the simmer – just enough to cover the rice.

Keep stirring gently and adding stock as it absorbs until the rice is cooked – it's done when it is tender but still *al dente*.

Now, off the heat, add the remaining butter and the parmesan and stir into the risotto. Taste and season with salt if necessary – your stock may have been seasoned enough to ensure you don't need any.

Rest the risotto with the lid on while you make a quick salad, and serve with extra parmesan, for sprinkling over.

ADVENTURES OF A TERRIBLY GREEDY GIRL

MODELS, MAYHEM AND MARTINIS...

10 Things I Learned in New York

1. You always find the freshest seafood in Chinatown. Truth. Which is perfect if you want to cook Thai prawns/squid/clams (delete as applicable) on the weekend. Take a bracing walk across the Brooklyn Bridge and turn right past TriBeca.

2. Skinning eels is not easy. Use a bathtub.

3. Always carry heels in your bag.

4. Always stand AGAINST THE SUBWAY WALL. Never enter AN EMPTY SUBWAY CAR.

5. Never make eye contact on public transport (actually, this is probably more like 4b, but hey-ho).

6. You cannot buy wine in the supermarket. It is usually kept in a liquor store. Behind bullet-proof glass. Especially in Brooklyn.

7. You can furnish your whole apartment from stoop sales and dumpsters. Not to mention the flea market at 26th and 6th. As long as you don't mind ending up with a gold velour sofa.

8. Most male models are NOT gay. But there's only so long you can stare at a pretty boy before you have to talk to him.

9. Les Halles and Anthony Bourdain saved me more than once – there's nothing like a rare steak and a pack of Marlboro Reds to help you deal with a vegetarian.

10. Living with a supermodel on the 49th floor in TriBeca is not conducive to making friends. Nor is having rather extraordinary black welts all over your limbs. I've got you now...

11. (Because, let's face it, 5 was really 4b) The only good thing to come out of *Sex and the City* was the Cosmopolitan.

10 THINGS I LEARNED IN NEW YORK

Lune's Prawns

My nanny Lune rarely cooked for us. When she did, she made simple things, usually when we were down at the beach bungalow in Pattaya. (She made the best chips I've ever had – better even than Jeremy Lee's at Quo Vadis, which is saying something. I still kick myself for not asking her secret...)

This is her method of cooking fresh prawns. It's incredibly simple, and makes the best I've ever had (with the possible exception of some grilled river prawns at a restaurant on the U-Thong Road in Ayutthaya).

FEEDS 2 GREEDY PEOPLE

1kg (2lb 4oz) prawns (shrimp), with   sea salt
    their shells on

Wash the prawns thoroughly in water. Put them into a pan with just the residual water clinging on to them. Throw in a good amount of salt – do not be shy with it!

Cover the pan with a tight lid and place over a medium heat for about 3 minutes or so, shaking a couple of times as you go. Then take off the lid to reveal plump, pink, juicy prawns that truly taste of the sea.

Pile them on to a plate, still steaming, and serve with a smile, a glass of Sancerre and a couple of dips – my favourites include sriracha sauce, the Nam Jim Seafood on page 40, or a fresh and pungent aïoli.

ADVENTURES OF A TERRIBLY GREEDY GIRL

MODELS, MAYHEM AND MARTINIS...

FORMOSA CAFE

ADVENTURES OF A TERRIBLY GREEDY GIRL

Meet Me at the Formosa...

(or These are a few of my favourite bars)

The Formosa Café, on Santa Monica Boulevard, is more than just a bar. It's Hollywood. Hollywood then; Hollywood now. It's the Hollywood where Elvis had a date with Marilyn and tipped the waitress with a Cadillac. It's the Hollywood where John Wayne would sleep off a heavy night and then cook the owner breakfast in the morning. It's the Hollywood where Faye Dunaway pops in for a quiet martini, and where Mickey Cohen kept a safe in the floor.

It was the last place Elizabeth Short, the Black Dahlia, was seen alive. It was the unofficial commissary for the Warner Hollywood lot next door. Its owner won it in a bet. It was the place you came to get a drink, buy your lunch, cash a cheque or place a bet and get a date.

Everyone who was anyone, and a whole bunch of no ones, has had a drink at the Formosa. Still it marks the time, a witness to the glamour of movie stars and the failed dreams of the hopefuls who never made it, a witness to the gangland crime that underpinned the golden age of the movie business.

It's a bar that (almost) never changes in a city where change is the only thing that stays the same. And it is my spiritual home. Walking into the dimly lit room from the bright LA sunshine makes you blink, makes you feel a little giddy. Then your eyes adjust and you realize that you've been transported back in time to an era of red-leather booths, wood and zinc bar-tops, dry martinis and drier humour. You're in Old Hollywood now, baby. Movie stars' portraits line the walls. Occasionally, they sit next to you.

I first walked in for a *Dumbo Drop* reunion. We'd been to a party for Danny Glover's stand-in (who'd also been Big Bird on *Sesame Street* – the fame) and were looking for a "somewhere next". John Bramley suggested here. (It's all his fault.) I was enchanted to the point where I became a regular. I'd turn up for a margarita just before closing. Then I'd order another. At first, Vince the owner tried to refuse me. But I would steal the keys and wouldn't let him lock up until he'd made me one. Terrible behaviour. But, then again, I had witnessed Vince bouncing ripped and hard-core stunt puppies, so I figured that if I was bothering him, he had ways and means to let me know. Instead, he'd make me my margarita in a pint glass and get on with cleaning up. It has proved the basis for a lasting friendship.

The Formosa was, to me, a perfect bar. Certainly, it was where I fell in love with bar culture. Before I moved to Los Angeles, drinking was something done at parties, in nightclubs or in pubs. Primarily in pubs. The World's End was just a hop and a skip from Models 1, the place we'd go to drink really shitty white wine, smoke Marlboro Lights, talk bollocks and stagger from shortly after 11pm.

Bars were very different to pubs. They still are. Maybe it's a cultural thing. Back in the day, you wouldn't dream of walking into a pub and ordering a martini. Let alone a margarita. Bars immediately seemed sophisticated, even if you were in a dive like the Frolic Room. More Raymond Chandler than Colin Dexter, if you know what I mean – mean streets versus dreaming spires. Just cooler.

Cocktails were resolutely out of fashion in the Britain I had left. Here in America, they weren't a question of fashion; they were as ubiquitous an order as a pint of best or a gin and tonic. You would expect a bartender to have a basic command of the classics. In as august and historic a dive as the Formosa, I couldn't help but take my first steps into cocktail culture, something that would eventually change my life.

I've spent a lot of time thinking about what makes a bar a good bar. With the Formosa, its sense of history was just a part of it. And I am biased towards it because it was, for me, the first bar where everybody knew my name. I think it boils down to one word: honesty. All my favourite bars are honest and true to themselves, and they do what they do *well*. Were I to single out a few, they would be these:

1. The Formosa Café, for all the reasons above.

2. The late, lamented Passerby in New York. Buried beside a hidden gallery in the Meatpacking District, Passerby sadly closed in 2008. But you can read all about it in owner Toby Cecchini's book *Cosmopolitan*. With its tiny room, flashing disco floor and exceptional collection of under-the-counter rums, it was as flawlessly true to Cecchini's vision of bar perfection as could be. It is not a coincidence that I haven't been back to Manhattan since it closed.

ADVENTURES OF A TERRIBLY GREEDY GIRL

3. Gleneagles. Overlooking the picturesque Mgarr harbour on the island of Gozo, this is earthy and unpretentious. Run by Tony and Sammy for as long as I can remember, I realize now that it is probably the first bar I ever visited. (For the record, I was five.) Despite its tourist-friendly positioning, it remains what it is supposed to be: a fishermen's bar, a place to drink and smoke, to talk or not talk after a hard day at the nets. The welcome is warm (God, I *hate* places like *An American Werewolf's* The Slaughtered Lamb, where everyone looks round at a stranger when they walk in), but it remains faithful to its core clientele. This is their place. You're very welcome, but you're just visiting.

4. Quo Vadis in London. This is not just another case of the "everybody knows my name" thing. The drinks are strong and the atmosphere louche. It's properly Soho. And it has Jeremy Lee. And Sam and Eddie Hart, who give good restaurant. I love, I love, I love.

5. Chez Jay. Oh, the stories this Santa Monica bar could tell! It was here that I met the man who took the purse to Kinshasa for the Rumble in the Jungle. It's here that they have the peanut Alan Shepard took to the moon. Here that the Secret Service stashed Marilyn before they drove her up the beach to Peter Lawford's house for assignations with John Kennedy. Sawdust on the floor, steaks and sand-dabs on the menu, crisp martinis... bring it on.

6. Dandelyan, overlooking the Thames in London. When you pop to the loo, they put your martini in the fridge *so it's still cold when you get back*. That's service. That's style. That's a way to a girl's heart.

7. Bar Termini in London's Soho. Postage stamp sized, but oh! So chic! Oh! So Italian! Oh! So Negroni!

But Formosa's where it started. One day, my ashes will rest here. In my pint glass. Next to the Elvis booth. Maybe my ghost can cook breakfast with John Wayne's before we scare the owners.

Formosa Café-style Pork Rib Tacos

The menu at the Formosa Café has been the subject of much debate among Angelenos over the years. But the one order everyone could agree on was the Chinese ribs, to which Vince has never given me the recipe. He did, however, make me an extraordinary carnitas fried rice – a brilliantly LA fusion of Mexican and Chinese food. This is not that recipe either. But it was its inspiration.

SERVES 4

1.5kg (3lb 5oz) baby back ribs, cut into 4 racks

For the barbecue sauce:

3 tablespoons thick soy sauce

3 tablespoons light soy sauce

4cm (1½ inch) piece of fresh root ginger, peeled and chopped

2 tablespoons sherry or Chinese rice wine

4 tablespoons hoisin sauce

4 garlic cloves, chopped

3 tablespoons tomato ketchup

2 tablespoons honey

a good pinch of chilli flakes (optional)

You will also need shredded lettuce, guacamole and good-quality corn tortillas.

First make the barbecue sauce. Place all the ingredients in a blender, and blitz until smooth. Set aside until needed.

Preheat the oven to 150°C (300°F), Gas Mark 2.

Trim the membrane off the bone side of the ribs. The easiest way to do this is by inserting the tip of a knife under the membrane, teasing it loose, then peeling

it off in a piece or two. (People tend to leave the membrane in place when they smoke racks of pork ribs, but removing it here makes for tender, falling apart ribs that are easy to shred on to your tacos.)

Line two baking trays with foil. Place the ribs, meat side down, on the foil and brush them generously with half the barbecue sauce. Cover the whole tray with more foil. Then bake in the oven for 2 hours.

Now turn up the oven to 180°C (350°F), Gas Mark 4. Uncover and turn the ribs, and baste with the remaining barbecue sauce. Then bake for a further 25–30 minutes.

Remove from the oven and allow to rest while you shred some lettuce, make a fresh guacamole (you can use the Korean Guacamole on page 150 if you like), and make the Pico de Gallo on the next page. Warm some corn tortillas, shred the pork from the bones, and serve with lots of cold beer and napkins.

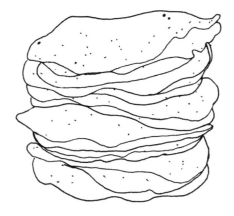

Pico de Gallo

Basically a fresh salsa – serve with anything grilled or eggs.

MAKES APPROXIMATELY 450G (1LB)

4–6 tomatoes, finely chopped

1 red onion, finely chopped

2 jalapeño chillies, deseeded and finely chopped

a handful of fresh coriander (cilantro) leaves, chopped

fresh lime juice, to taste

a good pinch of sea salt

Mix all the ingredients in a bowl and allow to sit for 10 minutes or so. Taste, adjust the seasoning, and serve.

ADVENTURES OF A TERRIBLY GREEDY GIRL

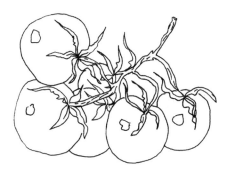

 125

MEET ME AT THE FORMOSA...

ADVENTURES OF A TERRIBLY GREEDY GIRL

What Would Martha Do?

In a world where things seldom go to plan, there is always Martha.

I was 18 years old when I bought my first Martha Stewart cookbook. It was 1982 and, up until then, all there had been on the shelf at home was Hamlyn's *All Colour Cookbook,* Delia Smith's *Cookery Course* and a slew of *Australian Women's Weekly* specials. All excellent but, let's be honest, less than glamorous.

Then along came Martha's *Entertaining.* With her glossy blonde locks and her frilly white New Romantic shirt, there she was, smiling seductively across a table laid with blue glass and poppies.

I was a smitten kitten.

I, too, would entertain like Martha. I, too, would make sure the place settings were just so, and the flowers matched the décor. What did it matter if she was in the bucolic surrounds of The Hamptons and I was in a small flat-share in Battersea? The chickens with their home-laid eggs might prove a bit of a stretch. But I could, I would BE Martha.

In times of crisis I turned to her: the piecrust's raw – what would Martha do? Don't panic, she says from deep within. Just wow them with the titbit that you brought the Meyer lemons in the curd filling from sunny California last week. Sod the crust, she says, just scoop out the insides and make like "it's deconstructed". Don't panic – stay in control.

It's not just the food, either. Martha has an answer to everything. She even takes the pain out of home décor with her own range of paints and linens. I painted my kitchen in New York in Hummingbird Blue, with Morning Fog accents. My sheets were K-Mart Stewart Sage, the walls Apple Green.

We can learn many things from Martha the Unruffled. After all, she's probably the only person ever who has managed to turn going to prison into A Good Thing™.

Here are some I prepared earlier:

1. Decorating your chicken coop should be encouraged.

2. Everyone should have a wrapping room. No, really. I mean, I don't. My wrapping paper is shoved into closets and drawers, and is re-used, slightly creased and tied up with string. Martha would probably wrinkle her nose at this, and then rebrand it Recycled Rustic.

3. Dry your decanters by inserting rolled-up snakes of kitchen towel to wick out the last of the damp. Because we all have A LOT of decanters.

4. Snoop Dog and Martha make the best brownies ever.

5. Martha can speak to the animals. She uses a special language. I rather fail at this – I give the animals far too many nicknames instead.

6. Leave yourself messages and reminders with Post-It notes all over the house. I LOVE a Post-It note. Martha colour coordinates hers with the décor.

In the clear light of day and with 30-plus years' worth of reflection, I have come to the blinding realization that I am more of a Julia than a Martha. With more of a five-minute rule than a five-second rule if I drop something (which really means "Forget about it, the dog's already eaten it..."). More of a "never apologize, never explain" kind of girl than a "don't panic – stay in control" chick. But, then again, when my inner Julia's been at the sauce, I can (and still do) ask: What Would Martha Do?

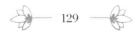

ADVENTURES OF A TERRIBLY GREEDY GIRL

A Baguette *Jambon Cru*
Can Save Your Life

I wasn't supposed to go to Cannes. In all my years in fashion, I'd never had to. Even when I worked in actual, proper film production, it was unnecessary. It was all Joan's fault.

The year before, Joan had rescued me from making the terrible mistake of staying in New York by offering me a job at IFG, a company that sold completion bonds (please don't ask... basically, it's insurance for film finance, but if you make me tell you, we'll be here for hours and hours and neither of us will especially enjoy it). At first, I turned her down. I knew nothing about film finance.

"You'll pick it up," she said. "You're a quick study."

I said I'd think about it. And now here I was, a year later, on the Croisette with aching feet, wishing I'd listened to Joan's one piece of Cannes advice: wear comfortable shoes.

The thing about Cannes is that it's really not about the films. It is instead a trade show, primarily about deals. If you're a film critic, you'll see films. If you're a programmer for another film festival, you'll see lots of films. If you're a buyer, you'll see lots of little bits of films. If you're an actor, you'll see your film. If you're a seller, you'll see little bits of your films over and over and over again. If you're anyone else with a Festival pass, you'll see the Majestic, the Carlton, the Grand, the bunker, bouncers, canapés, rope lines, hem lines, by-lines and more too-warm Provençal rosé than you could drink in a year. And all of it as you gallop, hot, sweaty and gasping, to The Next Meeting which started five minutes ago at the other end of the Croisette.

And I had been *so* looking forward to it.

Like everyone else, I'd been primed for Cannes by the pictures, the effortless "because you're worth it" glamour bathed in Côte d'Azur sunlight, Julianne Moore looking impossibly chic on the red carpet. Yes, it would be work, but I'd imagined myself tripping through it like Audrey Hepburn in *Roman Holiday*, rather than Bruce Willis in *Die Hard*.

So it was quite by chance that, with a 20-minute window between appointments, I happened upon the café of my dreams, tucked away on the Rue

du Commandant André: Caffè Lalu. A movie-biz-free zone. Oh, the bliss! Just the night before, I had attempted a romantic dinner with my boyfriend, only to be called by my London boss who'd failed to blag his way into his choice of that night's parties and was looking for something to do. He would never find me at Lalu's. These 20 minutes would be mine, all mine, undisturbed. Madame Lalu, who sat by the bar in a worn housecoat, would prepare me the freshest baguette *jambon cru*, served with *une pression*, and my life would be whole once more.

Lalu's became the perfect place, right at the heart of the Festival, to see Cannes for what it is. A trade show, yes, but one packed with tourists. I do not know why anyone would ever, *ever*, *EVER* go to Cannes as a tourist at Festival time. I have seen a bewilderbeast of paparazzi throw tourists into traffic just to snap another shot of Paris Hilton.

Which brings us neatly to the first other thing Cannes is about: sensation. Ever since Brigitte Bardot was "discovered" sunbathing in a bikini in 1953 and Simone Silva tried to one-up her by posing topless with Robert Mitchum on the beach the following year, the Festival has been the ultimate promotional opportunity, whether for yourself (Ms Hilton) or your movie. Only at Cannes would someone like Jerry Seinfeld choose to suspend himself on a zip wire dressed as a bee.

The stunts come and go. The constant is the next thing that Cannes is about: status. No other event lets you know your place in the picture-business hierarchy quite like it. Do you get to sit in the sun or the shade on the Carlton terrace? How long must you wait in the Majestic lobby before being ushered over to the Palais for your big moment? Even within IFG – a company that no longer exists since the Big Boss from Chicago, Mike Segal, who ran our underwriters the Fireman's Fund, was sent to jail on racketeering charges – our status was made plain. The US bosses stayed at the Eden Roc. Marvellous! Glamorous! Cash only! My London boss stayed at the Gray d'Albion. Not too shabby. Just up from the Majestic. Good for networking. I was placed at the Montfleury, with a 20-minute walk to the Croisette, and the host venue for the annual Hot d'Or Awards. The porn equivalent of the Palme d'Or, complete with a pink latex carpet and wipe-down furniture. Of an evening, the lobby was full of fascinating characters, not one of whom was making a film that we could bond. It always struck me, as someone not so *au fait* with porn, that some of the women were quite attractive, if a little too short and pneumatic for fashion. The men... not so much. Perhaps their talents lay elsewhere. Interestingly, their annual shindig seemed quite a staid affair. Unlike some of the Festival parties proper. Which brings me to the final thing that Cannes is about: parties.

Parties in Cannes are A Very Big Deal™. The *Hollywood Reporter* used to rank the main parties on a scale of zero to three martini glasses in the back of each issue of its *Festival Daily*. It becomes rather like Vegas after a while: what happens in Cannes stays in Cannes. People tend to act outside the normal realms of their behaviour. And they turn slightly feral when it comes to blagging passes and invites. Imagine, if you will, a game of Top Trumps played over breakfast at the Petit Majestic, accompanied by an aggressive hangover sharpened by lack of sleep: "Oh yes," says Player A, "I was at FilmFour, but then I *had* to go to the New Line thing at the Villa." "Really?" says Player B. "I didn't get to that. I was a guest on Werner Herzog's yacht where I threw up on [Roddy, Malcolm, Andie – delete as applicable, depending on vintage] MacDowell's shoes..."

I saw invite-blagging up close every year as we moved towards my company's annual lunch on the du Cap terrace, held as a thank you to everyone we'd had business with the year before. The hired PR mavens would move on to planning the next event the day before the lunch, forwarding my mobile number to every blagger, ligger and fly-by-night in southern France. Because every lawyer, financier, green-light guy (it's *always* a guy) and venture capitalist would be there to eat wild strawberry tarts while looking out over the Mediterranean. So, after three days of wall-to-wall appointments, Cannes Monday would find me in a crumpled heap on my hotel-room floor, on the phone, fending off grown men, elegant women and tomorrow's industry leaders, all demanding to know why THEY weren't on the list. All before meeting them face to face the next day as I was transformed into the World's Smallest Bouncer, armed with a clipboard, heels and a wrap dress to remind them of the answer.

No wonder Caffè Lalu was the answer to my dreams.

When I look back on Cannes's gone by, that baguette is the meal I remember. After all, you don't go to Cannes for the food. My LA bosses might regale me

with tales of "the most wonderful dinner we had at Le Moulin de Mougins with Mel Gibson last night"; I'd smile and say, "Great!" while thinking, "Thanks, I had a fucking midnight sandwich at the Montfleury surrounded by porn stars." That baguette. And sharing Joan's annual pilgrimage to a Breton crêperie in Juan-les-Pins the day after The Lunch.

A crêpe in Provence may not seem like the ideal choice, but I always looked forward to it, as I did to any down time I had to spend with Joan. More than anyone else in any of the businesses I've worked in, she was my mentor. She gave me my first proper job in film; she brought me back to Europe when I needed it the most. She pushed me hard and taught me not just to be better at my job, but to be a better woman too. She'd done it all. She was the surf betty who went on to become the cinematographer of Oscar-winning documentaries, who never let anyone in the film business tell her what she couldn't be just because she was a woman. And, of the three core pieces of advice she gave me – wear comfortable shoes in Cannes; never let them see you cry – the best remains: never assume – assumption is the mother of all fuck-ups.

She died ten years ago. I was in Malta, looking after my mother while Dad had heart surgery. I'd spoken to her a couple of months before on the phone, but she hadn't wanted to see me – she would have hated me to remember her in sickness. So I didn't. Instead, Fred and I went to a bar on the harbour, drank a lot of Irish whiskey in her honour, and told Joan stories. And he reminded me of the time she came to dinner and asked for the recipe afterwards even though she couldn't cook, but because she wanted to remember the meal. This, over the page, was it, clean *and* decadent, and definitely "Joan food".

ADVENTURES OF A TERRIBLY GREEDY GIRL

A BAGUETTE JAMBON CRU CAN SAVE YOUR LIFE

Poulet Noir dans son Jus

SERVES 4

1 × 1.5kg (3lb 5oz) chicken, ideally
a Poulet de Bresse but any good
free-range chicken will do

25g (1oz) butter

1 tablespoon olive oil

1 onion, quartered

1 carrot, roughly chopped

3 stalks of parsley

1 bay leaf

1 leek, roughly chopped

1 bulb of garlic, unpeeled but cut in
half horizontally

sea salt and freshly ground black
pepper

For the sauce:

285ml (9½fl oz) white wine

50g (1¾oz) butter

Preheat the oven to 180°C (350°F), Gas Mark 4.

Season the inside of the chicken with salt and pepper. Melt 25g (1oz) of butter with the oil in a casserole big enough to hold the chicken comfortably. (Failing that, you can use a roasting pan and cover it with foil to achieve the same effect – which I do when I double the recipe for a dinner party.) Add the onion, carrot, parsley stalks, bay leaf, leek and garlic. Then lay the chicken breast-down on the vegetables. Cover and cook in the oven for about 35 minutes. Then turn the bird over and cook for another 40 minutes or so, until cooked. To test it, stab the thickest part of the thigh with a skewer – the juices should run clear. Remove it from the pan and keep it warm.

Skim any chicken fat off the juices in the casserole, then add the white wine and bring to the boil. Reduce the liquor by half, then strain it through a sieve into a saucepan and season it with salt and pepper.

Discard the herbs and set the vegetables aside to keep warm. Technically, I think you're supposed to discard them, but they have so much flavour and the garlic especially is so good smeared on crusty bread that I always bring them to the table in a separate bowl so everyone can help themselves.

Gently bring the jus back to the heat without boiling, stirring in the remaining 50g (1¾oz) of butter in small bits to enrich the sauce until it has all melted.

Carve the chicken on to a warm serving plate and pour a couple of serving spoons of the jus over the top.

Serve at once with the rest of the jus and the vegetables on the side, ideally with a simple green salad and plenty of good French bread.

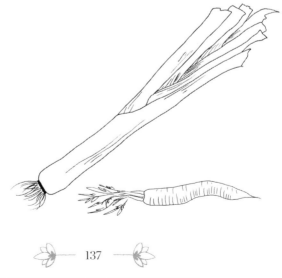

A BAGUETTE JAMBON CRU CAN SAVE YOUR LIFE

ADVENTURES OF A TERRIBLY GREEDY GIRL

The Art of the Party

I do love a cocktail party. I consider it the apogee of entertaining, an effortless affair of drinks and snacks where guests in the sharpest suits, the chicest dresses, laugh and mingle on a balmy summer night.

My parents threw many such parties, twisting the Bangkok night away on the terracotta terrace, the music drifting through the palm trees, as I, like Sabrina (in the Audrey Hepburn film, not *The Teenage Witch*...), peered out through the shutters and longed to be part of it. Alas, my one attendance at one of these parties did not go quite as I'd planned. I was watching through the bannisters, wrapped in my towel, still pink from my bath, when I tried to move to a better vantage point... and slipped... all the way down the stairs, arriving at the party a naked bundle of white-hot embarrassment to howls of guestly mirth.

Well, a girl has to learn how to make an entrance.

Naked appearances notwithstanding, I rather miss the conviviality of the old ways. I miss the effortlessly shaken cocktails, the silk shirts and the stylish frocks, the fact that people danced to the band instead of ignoring it. Mine may be a quixotic campaign, but I want to see the cocktail party restored to its proper glory in our lives. And all because, as my Mum used to say, I have gin in my veins: I was conceived *en route* from Bangkok to London after she and my Dad had put away round after round of contraband Tom Collins, served discreetly in teapots, back in the day when Bombay was a dry port and everyone knew what a Tom Collins was.

As a result, I now have a bit of a problem: whenever anyone comes to the house, they expect my bar to be fully stocked for almost any cocktail they can imagine. It is not. Especially if Fred's been at the rum. But it makes me realize that a cocktail party can seem like a daunting affair for those of us whose budget doesn't run to a full bar service. So, in order to promote my quixotic scheme, here are my top tips for hosting a good cocktail party of your own:

1. Planning is all. A good party is like a swan on the water – you want people to see it glide along with effortless cool; you don't want them to notice the effort. And it will take some effort. But if you plan well, the effort will take care of itself. You can get the booze in well in advance or, even better, have it delivered. Make sure there's plenty of ice. Cocktails demand it, and you

can never have too much. And (shock-horror! How could a food writer say such a thing?!) you can buy food in. By all means, make *some* – bang out a few crab cakes or a paté – but don't feel you have to. You can find perfectly delicious tarts or charcuterie at the deli. It all depends on this: what's your thing? If you're all about the food, major on that, and keep the drinks simple. If you're all about giving your friends a good time, take the pressure of preparation off as much as possible. Good planning is about knowing your limits, because –

2. Relax. This is a party. You're hosting the damned thing to have fun and, more importantly, to give fun. So no one wants a frazzled, snappy, stressed-out hostess on their hands. If you're relaxed, you can –

3. Be a good host. I think hosting a party is a great forgotten art. Great parties are well hosted. A good host doesn't just make sure you have a drink, and they certainly don't say, when Bob arrives, "Hey, Bob – this is everyone. Everyone, this is Bob!" If poor Bob doesn't know anyone there, he's going to need to be extremely socially confident, and even the *most* socially confident have bad days when they want to recuse themselves to the spare room and quietly wibble. Have a clear idea of the people that would like to meet Bob and that Bob would like to meet. Steer him to them. Then he can take care of himself.

The art of hosting cannot be overestimated. Even into retirement, my folks carried on entertaining. My mother *loved* a party; and my Dad had a Little Black Book in which he kept track of who drank what (very handy for the planning, above) *and* what to look for if they were getting too pissed. If you think about it, this is where bar-keeping and party-throwing connect. I knew a bartender once – she was as sweet as toffee and twice as brittle, if you get my drift – who really *knew* her patrons. She knew what they drank, what they liked and what they didn't like, as all great bartenders should. You can see this skill in the way they remember names, the way their eyes scan the room. They know what's going on, always. The lighting is flattering. The drinks are cold. And they never run out of ice. Putting the maths to one side for a second, this is the heart of the hospitality business. And it's the heart of hosting a good party, too. It never hurts to watch a really good barsmith in action. Take notes. The key difference, of course, is that any old fool can wander into a bar; at your party, they're there by invitation. Which brings us to –

4. Casting. The worst dinner party I ever held wasn't an abject failure because of the food (I have served up some shockers before now, but in those cases the evenings have at least turned out to be entertaining...), it was because I had forgotten that two of the guests had had a disastrous affair a couple of years prior. Silent fury and recrimination, it turns out, are no good for anyone's digestion. At a cocktail party, there's a certain safety in numbers. And, of course, you cannot be expected to know every detail of your guests' various pasts. But if you know that you can't put two or more of your chums in the same room at the same time, you really shouldn't.

5. Follow your own style. It is, after all, your party, and you *can* cry if you want to. For what it's worth, my style seems to have evolved into a blend of Asian and modern. I had a serious vintage phase that bordered on kitsch for a while. I love collecting glassware. And I think an Arne Jacobsen-designed cocktail shaker is essential. Even though it's not really a shaker (if you tried, you'd spray your drink all over the walls), it is the ideal vessel for stirring the perfect martini.

6. And the most important thing? Enjoy yourself. If the quiche hits the floor, there's always the five-second rule. Or Deliveroo. So, as Elizabeth Taylor would say, pour yourself a drink, put on some lipstick and pull yourself together. It's supposed to be a party.

ADVENTURES OF A TERRIBLY GREEDY GIRL

An English Cook
in a California Kitchen

In America, I learned to let go of the rules. In lots of ways. And especially in cooking. It was the moment when I realized how to use the East/West dichotomy of my upbringing and my palate to my advantage. In Bangkok, I saw different food cultures side by side every day. In Los Angeles, I was seeing it all over again. And I learned to go out on a limb, to try combinations that might seem odd at first, but that my gut told me would work. Like Korean tacos. Or Vietnamese gumbo. And I realized that it's the blessing of a new country: recent immigrants and second-generation citizens can reclaim their food heritage in America and move it forward into something new. It's not so much a food fusion as a food evolution. And in a town like LA, it happens fast – every day.

Years ago, I tried to explain the idea of the Palate of My Imagination and My Memory™ (Imagine if you will, a book – the word PALATE inscribed on the spine. The words My Imagination on one cover. My Memory on the other. Thank you.) to my then agent. She didn't get it. A few years later I tried to explain it to my publisher. She didn't get it, either. So now, dear readers, come on a journey with me to learn what I mean.

This kind of cookery is not always about following a recipe. It's not always about making a shopping list. It's about trusting your memory and your imagination – your palate – and allowing it to guide you. It can be freeing.

Let's imagine together. It's a Sunday. A gloriously cornflower-blue October day at the Hollywood Farmers' Market. There's live music playing, dogs yapping, kids fighting, street food sizzling, and there's row upon serried row of unforgettable produce. We've strolled over from the house we're renting in Whitley Heights to see what we can find.

There's some Scots kale – let's steam and wilt that down and serve it with a fava bean purée, like we had on our honeymoon in Puglia. The memory of a dish meets an ingredient in the market, and already we know what we want to do with it. Here are Meyer lemons. What magnificent specimens! They are small and round with a smooth skin hiding the sweetest lemon juice you have ever tasted, with an almost bergamot-scented finish. They're a hybrid of a true lemon and a mandarin or sweet orange, originally cultivated in China and introduced to the USA by Frank Meyer in the 1900s. (I used to have a romantic notion that it was actually called the Maya lemon and was named after some beautiful, tragic heroine of the Wild West... but no, it was made by an agriculturalist.) Meyers make the perfect preserved lemons, with just a pinch of saffron. Or a curd pie. Lemonade with a dash of basil and a splash of gin. The imagination, fired by a new ingredient, runs riot, offering up all kinds of possibilities.

Peacock kale – I'll sauté that with garlic and pine nuts. Then there are those big, scaly avocados and smaller smooth ones being sold for 50 cents to a buck each, ready to be mashed into guacamole or churned into ice cream with *pepitas* and chilli. Green tomatoes or tomatillos – I'll make salsa with those, or slice them and dip them in cornmeal, and fry them crisp to serve with a fat, pungent aioli. Heirloom tomatoes grown by an elderly Italian couple with seeds they brought from their homeland in the 1940s – huge and gnarled and almost black, but tasting as only tomatoes grown with love and ripened by the sun can taste. There's no other place my imagination can take me with those than to make a rich, deep tomato sauce to pop in the freezer for quick pastas. Asian herbs and chillies of every shape and size – I'll pickle some of the chillies and use the herbs to make a fresh green dressing for fish.

Then there's the fruit: apples and pears, perfect for spiced crumbles or streusels; large, late, sunset-hued peaches, ready to be roasted with amaretti or churned with basil into a sorbet; sugar-sweet saffron-coloured persimmons – perfect with a chunk of feta, crumbled with mint and coriander and just a spritz of olive oil; and wonderful pregnant pomegranates, virtually splitting and spilling over with seed and juice – a pomegranate Bellini comes to mind. There's late-harvest asparagus just pleading to be steamed, and every shade of autumn represented in the legion of pumpkins and squash, bringing thoughts of spiced pumpkin brûlées or a warming squash soup.

It's been said before, but it bears repeating, California is all about the produce. Not for nothing was it called the "Cornucopia of the West". For an English cook like me, who's learned to make a virtue of the extremes of British seasons and not to trust supermarket soft fruit in the winter, the possibilities are almost limitless. Inspiration lurks on every market stall.

ADVENTURES OF A TERRIBLY GREEDY GIRL

Take purslane, for instance. This is something I'd only read about in pre-war English cookbooks and in some Mexican tomes as *verdilago*. It's a prolific grower, a weed in all but name, and it's delicious – a bit like a fatter, juicier, sweeter watercress. And it has more Omega-3 content than salmon. Furthermore, it's more robust than watercress, so surely it could survive for a little while at the greengrocer's back home, and yet in London I never see it. Here, I toss some of it together with wild dandelion leaves, and dress it with Meyer lemon juice and extra virgin olive oil. And with the rest, a tempura batter beckons; I serve it crisp with a tamari-sesame oil dip.

The joy of a city like Los Angeles is its diversity. In London, I have a tendency to be lazy, to go to the same places time and again. In Los Angeles, as a frequent visitor, I want to explore. For it is a city rich with diverse ingredients. In Bangkok Plaza in Thai Town, Hollywood, I can buy, among other goodies, live blue crabs for a dollar each. Yes, I said a dollar. There are Persian shops in Westwood for wonderful yogurts, feta and herbs for *sabzi*. There's Little Ethiopia rubbing shoulders with the kosher Jewish delis on Fairfax (my idea of pickle heaven), Chinatown for great seafood and arguably the freshest poultry I've ever bought.

At the east end of the city, in its historic Downtown area, lies the Grand Central Market. It has changed a lot in recent years due to local development and gentrification. Back when I first started shopping there, using the newly opened subway to ride Downtown from Hollywood, it was mostly a Hispanic market with Asian overtones. Here I saw one morning a chap eating breakfast at a Chinese food stall, adding sliced onions, tomatillos and a chipotle salsa to his pork stir-fry. Organic fusion with a crash and a bang, in real time.

Here, too, I began my ever-continuing education in Mexican food, thanks to stallholders who would generously give their time to explain how to use their home-made *mole* pastes or the subtle differences between particular dried chillies. Here, therefore, my approach as a cook needs to change. No longer is this simply about ingredients. It's now about learning about another food culture. And while we can play all we want with flavours and textures and recipes, food is inextricably tied to culture. Here I see again how food, if we are open to it and the people who make it, readily unlocks a window into other

AN ENGLISH COOK IN A CALIFORNIA KITCHEN

cultures. People want to explain what they eat, how they eat and why they eat certain things in certain ways. And we can find the pure forms of regional cooking and culture from all over Central America whenever we choose to look for it.

But still in LA, food cultures constantly nudge and elbow up against each other in a way I haven't seen in Britain. Maybe I'm going to the wrong places. But I find that, if I want excellent Jamaican ingredients, I go to Brixton; if I want particular Indian ingredients, I go to Southall. And so on. And there, I am all but immersed in those cultures for a couple of hours. But in the Hollywood or Santa Monica farmers' markets, I can walk Thai stalls, regional Mexican stalls, Santa Barbara fishermen's stalls, date stalls from Indio, Korean stalls, Japanese stalls, all selling their ingredients in the same market at the same time. It's like a glorious cymbal smash of culture and flavour that's alive with possibility. And that drive for reinvention that, for me, defines America, ensures that all these Americans, new and old, will keep pushing forward, creating cuisines anew. In one walk through the market on this perfect autumn Sunday, I feel I can, too.

ADVENTURES OF A TERRIBLY GREEDY GIRL

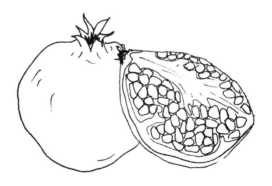

AN ENGLISH COOK IN A CALIFORNIA KITCHEN

Avocado Ice Cream

I remember when I first went to a California farmers' market. The abundance of both citrus and avocados – ripe avocados at that – astonished me. I was in heaven. After making a hundred iterations of guacamole, I had to make this, a combination that is just sunshine on a plate.

MAKES 750ML (ABOUT 1¼ PINTS)

400ml (14fl oz) milk

150g (5½oz) caster (superfine) sugar

4 ripe avocados

1 tablespoon lime juice

250ml (9fl oz) double (heavy) cream

dried chilli flakes or powder (optional)

toasted sunflower seeds or *pepitas* (optional)

sea salt (optional)

Gently heat the milk and sugar in a small saucepan until the sugar has dissolved. Do not allow to boil. Remove from the heat and allow to cool completely.

When completely cold, halve the avocados, remove the stones and scoop the flesh into a blender with a spoon. Add the lime juice and the milk mixture. Whizz until smooth.

Remove from the blender and place in a cold bowl. Add the double cream and stir well to combine. Pop into the fridge for about 40 minutes, until very cold.

Place in an ice-cream maker and churn until done.

Serve sprinkled with a little dried chilli, salt and toasted sunflower seeds or *pepitas*, if you like.

ADVENTURES OF A TERRIBLY GREEDY GIRL

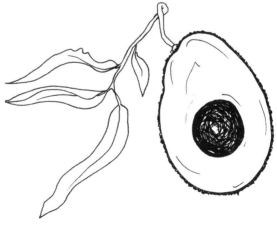

Korean Guacamole with Chicharrones

Here's a little more avocado love with a K-Town topspin. You will need to start making the *chicharrones* 2 days in advance.

For the chicharrones or pork scratchings:

as much pork skin as your butcher will give you (you can always supplement with corn tortillas)

vegetable oil, for deep-frying

sea salt

For the Korean guacamole:

2 garlic cloves

3 large or 4 smaller ripe avocados, peeled and de-stoned

juice of ½ lime

2 heaped tablespoons kimchi, drained and finely chopped

a small handful of fresh coriander (cilantro), chopped

sea salt

Bring a large pan of salted water to the boil. Place the pork skin in the pan. Bring back to the boil and cook for about 60–90 minutes, until fork tender.

Remove the skin from the pan with a slotted spoon. Allow to cool on a rack for 5–10 minutes, until cool enough to handle.

Using a tablespoon, scrape as much fat as you can off the skin. Place the skin on a baking tray and place in the fridge for at least 3 hours, or overnight if possible.

Preheat the oven to 50°C (120°F), Gas as low as it will go. Place the skin in the oven for 24 hours, turning every now and then. When the skin is done it should be almost see through – a bit like a stained-glass window. Remove from the oven and set aside to cool. Then break or crack the skin into small pieces.

Meanwhile, make the Korean guacamole. In a large *molcajete* or pestle and mortar, grind the garlic to a paste with a pinch of salt. Add the avocado and pound/mash until incorporated but still with some texture. Add a little of the lime juice. Add the kimchi and stir. Now stir through the coriander. Taste and adjust the seasoning, then set aside.

150

Heat oil in a wok over a medium heat until very hot. A cube of bread should crisp up and brown within 30 seconds. Or use a deep-fat fryer and heat the oil to 180°C (350°F).

Place the pieces of skin into the hot oil a few at a time. They will start to puff up immediately. Turn them and watch carefully. When they are golden and puffed up, remove with a slotted spoon or mesh net and set aside to drain on kitchen paper. Salt immediately.

Serve with the guacamole.

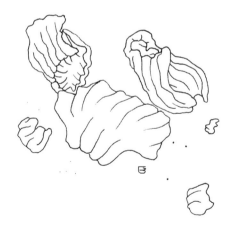

10 Things I Would Ban...
If I Were the Boss

1. **Mobile Phones**
   Look, I know we would all be lost without our mobiles. But please, people: can't we instil a little MPE (Mobile Phone Etiquette)? There are RULES. *My* rules. But rules nonetheless.

   a. Anyone who stands in doorways or tube exits and entrances on their phone deserves punishment.

   b. Anyone texting while driving? Punishment.

   c. Talking loudly on a plane, train or any other confined space? Big punishment.

   d. Checking phone at the dinner table unless you have pre-warned your dining companions (it had better be bloody important)? Defenestration.

2. **Men Who Spend Longer on Grooming than You Do**
   You can't trust them. Men with shaped eyebrows? Don't get me started. A little gentle taming is fine. I've been know to pull the strays out of Fred when he starts to get a little too Denis Healey. But the whole arched, shaped girl-brow on a man? Just no. Not unless your drag name is Bianca.

3. **"I'm on a Journey"**
   I wish I knew who coined the joke that you should never use the phrase "reach out" unless you're a member of the Four Tops. This cliché belongs in the same category. Enough, already. If you've been on a bus, on a plane, on a train, in the car... hell, if you've been for a walk, you've been on a journey. If you have been on *The X Factor*, you have not. Shut up and sing.

4. **The Clean-Eating Brigade**

Or "the wellness crowd", call them what you will. What they're peddling seems to come around cyclically. Last time, It was Gillian McKeith poking through our poo without proper qualifications. This time, it's a bunch of young hotties with blogs and Instagram accounts, flaunting their competitive and ostentatious healthiness, their message: "To look like me, you have to eat like me." Really? REALLY? Since when did these women – and they are primarily women, which has to say *something* about our total lack of self-esteem – get their degrees in nutritional therapy? Where did they study? What illnesses have they recovered from? They all seem to have had one. At least. What scientific basis do they have for what they're selling? What the hell is a spiralizer doing in anyone's kitchen drawers? And, while we're on about it, what the hell is "wellness"? It used to be called "watching what you eat" before someone ponced it up and slapped it on a blog. Yes, good nutrition matters. Yes, a proper diet is the key to health. But this is all cant, and some of it is actively dangerous. And it's another example of our media industry presenting young women with an unattainable body image to sell them shit off the back of their own now-growing lack of self-confidence. Let me tell you now: if you have a wellness blog and you aren't photogenic, I'm sorry, kid, those wellness big bucks ain't gonna come for you. Eat your greens. Enjoy the odd bacon sandwich. Avoid the "healthy" smoothie that seems to be good for you but is really packed with sugar. Be happy.

5. **People Who Call Themselves "Chef" when They Haven't Earned It**

If you can cook and serve tasty food for your friends, if you can manage catering an event for, say, up to 50 people, maybe even up to 100 with a little help, congratulations: you are a good cook. And that is an achievement. If you have peeled ten times your body weight in potatoes, pipped bushels of cherries, washed pots and pans until the early hours, been shouted at, burned by the grill until you have no hair on your

10 THINGS I WOULD BAN...IF I WERE THE BOSS

forearms, can work out the gross profit needed to keep your place afloat, have created new menus, worked 18-hour days, haven't slept in the same bed as your partner for months, and can only picture your parents behind one of your own restaurant tables, then you are a chef. Please, please do not confuse the two. I am a good cook. I ran a catering business, but I would never ever deign to call myself a chef. I'm not. And that is totally fine. Why a lot of cooks, especially those in the public eye, feel the need to call themselves chefs, I do not know. What's with wearing the chefs' whites, guys?

None of the following really rather excellent cooks have ever called themselves chefs: Elizabeth David, Jane Grigson, Ina Garten, Diana Henry, Nigella Lawson, Delia Smith, Julia Child, Marcella Hazan. They are cooks. They are communicators. And proud of it. They are brilliant. And they will all admit (not so much the dead ones) that chefs are a very different breed.

6. **Scooters in Supermarkets, Adults on Scooters or Skateboards Anywhere, Cyclists on the Pavement**

I have covered several modes of transport above, for all are ridiculous. I cannot count the number of times I have been tripped up by mama's little angel while bagging up my plums. All supermarkets should create a scooter park for these kids and charge them X amount of their pocket money to use it, or else be leashed up to the railings outside. Trust me – they'd use their legs then.

And adults... why? WHY? You're not Travis from *Clueless*. You're not retaining any youthful charm. You look foolish. You're in my way. And, did I say – you look foolish?

And cyclists? You should know better. And if you can't handle riding your bike on the road *like you're supposed to,* you should not be allowed on a bike at all.

Off with your heads.

ADVENTURES OF A TERRIBLY GREEDY GIRL

7. **(Most) Men in Tight V-Necks and Skinny Jeans**
    It may seem that this column is coming off a little sexist... it's just that
    I have certain issues with men's grooming (see point 2). So let's talk about
    skinny jeans, and here I mean the REALLY skinny ones that just look
    peculiar on most men. Their usually flat bottoms sort of sag a bit, pulled
    down by the skinniness on the lower leg. They look like Blackadder
    without the cod piece and the sense of humour. Now, I admit it, we girls
    have made our fashion faux pas over the years. None of us looked good in
    Katharine Hamnett's orange parachute-silk boiler suits except, maybe,
    Yasmin Le Bon. But it was just a phase we were going through. Skinny
    jeans on men, your time is up. Ditto tight, low-cut V-necks (ehem, Jude
    Law, are you listening?). It just seems a bit... desperate. Not to mention
    chilly. Is that why you have to wear that damned woolly beany at the same
    time? Stop, in the name of scruff. Enough is enough.

8. **Waiters Saying, "Hey, Guys!"**
    I'm all for Loving Your Waiter. Being rude to front-of-house restaurant
    staff comes pretty high on my list of social taboos. (I'd go so far as to say
    that I think a three-month (minimum) stint in a restaurant or bar should
    be obligatory for everyone who'd ever like to go to one.) But then, so too is
    this kind of weird over-familiarity that saw one waiter, *whom I'd never met*,
    pulling up a chair to join our table of six. Uninvited. In LA, I sort of expect
    some cheesy conversation, maybe even a script or a head-shot being pulled
    out of an apron pocket, because sometimes it's the only way to meet agents
    and casting directors. I'm not asking for a return to the old bowing and
    scraping "sir and modom (sic)" sort of service. A cheery "Hello there"
    works for me. "Hey, guys!" grates. Still more so if the "guys" lasts for more
    than a second.

9. **Onesies on Adults**
    Just odd. Actually peculiar. People wearing these border on being Plushies
    (if you need to ask, look it up). Who goes out dressed like that? It's as if you
    have a big sagging diaper under your bottom. Speaking of which, I did once

hear of cocktail fancy-dress parties in Yangon back in the day where the guests were invited to come dressed as babies, complete with diapers, appropriate head gear and so on, and received their cocktails of choice in their own personal giant bottle complete with nipple. But the Onesie is just wrong...

10. Pigeons

I'm not talking about homing pigeons. And I know there are people who love them. But when your flat has endured an infestation of the feral bastards and the run from the pavement from your front door used to be like the worst night of the Blitz but with shit, their demise cannot come soon enough.

And the One Rule I Would Instigate
Three-Martini Lunches

Because they are a joy and they make all the stuff above roll off my back like water off the proverbial duck's. Then again, if the martini isn't made *just right* ...

10 THINGS I WOULD BAN...IF I WERE THE BOSS

ADVENTURES OF A TERRIBLY GREEDY GIRL

Crying Tigers, Flying Ants
and a Snake Called Sid

Crying Tiger (seua long hai) *is a Thai dish with a story – it is grilled beef served with a hot-sour dip. I will tell the story below.*

I was supposed to be editing and testing a Thai cookbook for a large, successful, but rather money-conscious publisher. The deal got nixed (see "money-conscious"), but the place I had booked in Thailand for a month – all the better to source ingredients and cook in situ – could not be cancelled. I had found it online, and it looked to be a charming property on the coast, away from tourists, with a gas cooker and "a beautiful breeze that circulates cool air around the house, avoiding the need for air-conditioning". It was supposed to be the show home for a new development that would nestle in a valley a short walk from the beach.

It looked lovely.

And there's a chump born every minute.

Hello.

Day 1

The signs were there from the start. We drove past the turning twice. The first time, it was a case of "blink and you'll miss it"; the second a case of "no... it can't be." But it was: a dirt road leading to the property pitted with axle-breaking holes, overhung with bees' nests and draped in a torn and sagging banner reading "*wAlcomme*". The housekeeper's house, a shanty, was mere yards from the front door, obscuring the view entirely. And, I couldn't help but notice, it was in a sorry state. Especially for a housekeeper. There was a sad-looking dog chained to a fence and two smaller, emaciated pups running around. Pulling myself upright, I knocked on the housekeeper's door. With a sigh and a roll of her eyes, she let us into the property, exclaiming loudly that she didn't come in every day. "Good," I thought.

Things went further downhill at dusk. As the sun snapped off at 6.30 on the dot, the newborn night was filled with every flying, biting, stinging and crawling creature on God's great earth, both inside and out. The fly screens were all but useless as the living room became the entomological version of the cantina scene in *Star Wars*. The happy creatures with fewer than six legs were the *chinchoks*, little local geckos with huge Buddha bellies, for whom the dinner bell had now tolled.

Sleeping was tough without air-conditioning and without fans. We had to keep the bugs out, so we dared not open a window. And then there was the scurrying. A scratching in the eaves. Not one to be afraid, I switched on the torch and explored. Never before had I seen such creatures. They seemed like rats, but not as we know them. They had curly fur and piercing amber eyes. They only came out at night. There seemed to be a lot of them, swinging like rodent Tarzans through the climbing vines that had made the veranda look so enticing in the online brochure, and squeezing under the roof.

Our fresh eggs were gone in the morning.

Day 2

Bleary-eyed and sleep-deprived, I stumbled into the bathroom to see something green on the floor. At first I thought it must be a rolled-up towel. But then, mid-cleaning my teeth, I thought, "Wait a minute... why would there be a rolled-up towel on the floor?" And it moved.

Now, I'm not sporty. But, Pocahontas-like, I ran like the wind.

Snakes. Why did it have to be snakes?

Luckily, there was another bathroom, because we never ventured into that one again. Sid, as I christened him, had the tub all to himself...

Days 3–5

Fred had over a hundred bites on his arse. I counted them all. I even photographed them, such was my amazement. The maid had started dressing her two very sweet children in their Sunday best and sending them over to ask if we would buy them laptops or a car because we were foreign and "obviously rich". There was a strange smell wafting down the valley, which turned out to be a large swamp, the birthplace of our dear mosquito friends and no doubt the reason this development remained without buyers. With the smell of the swamp worsening, we had to leave.

Fortunately, we already had a road trip planned. It was all part of the research

160

for the now-not-my book. So we set off for Isaan, the far northeastern corner of the country, where we could have our revenge by eating bugs instead of being on the menu ourselves.

We ended up in a town called Buachet, not far from the Cambodian border, just across from the Phra Viharn temple, a historic site that at the time was the subject of a territorial dispute between Thailand and Cambodia. Oh, yes: in fleeing the bugs, we'd taken shelter by a war zone. But, all told, the gunshots at night were less annoying than the bastard biting insects back in Pranburi.

We arrived on the day of William and Kate's wedding, and were immediately and excitedly welcomed by a local village family, thrilled to have genuine British people in town for the occasion. They invited us to watch the proceedings on their 50-inch plasma screen, and together we toasted the happy couple with *lao khao* – a white alcohol made from rice that comes in almost spherical clay pots, the effects of which are like slamming your head in a car door. Repeatedly.

Our *lao khao* addlement was quickly compounded when we found the house where we were to stay. It looked like a Swiss chalet. All it needed was snow-capped mountains and Fred and me dressed in reindeer sweaters. Instead, it was set upon a manicured lawn which had been carved out of the forest.

It had been built by a lovely young man called Todd, a friend of a friend, who was from the village but now lived in Bangkok running a gay travel agency. It was appointed beautifully and – BLISS – the air-conditioning worked.

Todd and his Thai family came and spent some time with us, cooking, eating and inducting us into the bug-eating culture of the northeast. Now, before you turn your nose up, reader, bear in mind that eating bugs in northern Thailand is no different from eating *pied et paquets* – sheep's feet and stuffed tripe – in southern France. Both are cases of making the best of what you have available. And, up here, in Isaan, a dry and rural area with no tourist revenue to speak of, where people still live a subsistence way of life, nothing is wasted. Silk worms, for example, once they have spun out their silk, are steamed or just plunged into boiling water to blanch. Then they're served with a chilli-rich relish. They're surprisingly delicious – fatty and juicy.

We shouldn't be surprised. Bugs are an excellent source of sustainable

161

protein and, when treated right, they're pretty darn tasty. Perhaps getting used to the crunch of the exoskeleton is the biggest challenge. That, and removing legs and wings from your teeth. But it's a challenge we should meet instead of backing away in disgust.

And so, in the market, Todd and I bought water bugs, which we de-limbed and cooked in a beautiful sour curry to offset their crunch and buttery sweetness, and red ants' eggs. These are chubby and white, and far bigger than you'd think. They are springy, like firm salmon roe, and appear most frequently in a dish called *yum mot dang*, or red ant-egg salad. It's sharp and hot, and pleasingly nutty.

My favourite bug dish – one I'll seek out – is a snack called *rot duan*, which translates as "express trains". They're small bamboo worms, fried until crisp and served seasoned with salt and dried chilli. They taste very much like Ready Salted Chipsticks.

(By now you may be wondering if there's anything I won't eat. If I'm honest, I'm not wild about tripe. That said, on this trip, there was one thing that... well... we stopped at a roadside stall to see what was cooking – the source of some of my best Thai food experiences. The lady was selling frog. On a stick. Teeth intact and grimacing. She was amused to see the little Thai-speaking *farang* try one. Pretty tasty, if a tad tough – it might have been better hot. So then she showed me a jute sack she had in the shade, told me to trust her and shoved my hand inside it. It felt like a bag of testicles. Warm. Wriggling. Slightly creepy. And then I peered inside. To see pale, terrified, pregnant frogs. Ready to be blanched and grilled, *entier*. Bork! It is the one dish I drove away from as fast as I could.)

Buachet was a funny place. It is a rather pretty village set around a central covered market square. But I noticed the distinct lack of young people. There were lots of older people and lots of children, but no age groups in between. But this is Isaan, the rural heart of Thailand, where the dry seasons are long and hot and tough. I discovered that the average age of a farmer in the region now is 55. The younger generation don't want that life. So they move to the big city to drive taxis or tuk-tuks, or to work in construction, food stalls and bars. A huge percentage of the girls end up working in the sex trade. And almost all of them

ADVENTURES OF A TERRIBLY GREEDY GIRL

send their children home to be raised by mum and dad.

I love Isaan and her people. I love the culture, its connection to an older way of Thai life. I especially love the food, fierce and fiery, and yet with brilliantly controlled and structured flavours. The Thai Tourist Authority has been trying to rebrand the region, naming it the Emerald Triangle for the glorious green you see spread across it as the new rice grows in. It is difficult for foreigners up here – there's not a lot of English spoken, still less French or German or Swedish or Russian. But the rewards for the brave explorer are bountiful. The Khmer temples at Phi Mai and Buriram are glorious, but I have never seen another *farang* at either. And the food... well... not all of it features bugs. After all, *som tum* comes from here. And so do the following recipes.

Seua Long Hai

Grilled beef with a spicy dipping sauce

This recipe's name translates as "Crying Tiger" or "The Tiger Cried" and, as you can imagine, there are many tales of how it came by it. Some say that the dish comes from Isaan, where tigers used to roam freely. One day, some local villagers were grilling meat on the fire when the tigers smelt it. They crept from the forest, chased off the villagers, and gobbled up all the meat... all except for one slow tiger, who missed out and slunk back to the forest, sobbing and hungry.

Others say a tiger stole beef that had been dipped in this sauce, and it was soooo spicy that he wept with pain. This one, I believe!

Whichever is true, this recipe is quick, simple and delicious. And soooo spicy.

SERVES 2, OR 4 AS PART OF A LARGER MEAL

1 × 400g (14oz) sirloin steak

1 tablespoon soy sauce

1 teaspoon vegetable oil

For the nam jim jao:

3 tablespoons *nam pla* (fish sauce)

3 tablespoons lime juice

1–2 tablespoons roasted ground chilli powder

1 tablespoon finely chopped fresh coriander (cilantro)

2 small Thai shallots or 1 larger shallot, finely sliced

Marinate the steak in the soy sauce and vegetable oil for 15 minutes or so.

Heat a grill pan until you can feel the heat rising on to your hand when held 10cm (4 inches) above it – we want it HOT!

Pop the steak on the grill pan and cook it to your liking – about 8 minutes in all for medium. Set it aside to rest for another 5–10 minutes.

Meanwhile, mix together all the ingredients to make up the *nam jim jao* dipping sauce.

Slice the steak thinly and serve on a plate with the dipping sauce on the side.

CRYING TIGERS, FLYING ANTS AND A SNAKE CALLED SID

Gaeng Ohm

This is one of my very favourite things, a vegetable-heavy stew packed with dill and chillies. This version is based on a recipe from journalist and restaurateur Jarrett Wrisley, who runs, among other places, Soul Food Mahanakorn on Soi Thonglor in Bangkok. He in turn got it from A-Nong, a northern Thai friend of his. It captures the flavours of northeastern Thailand in a bowl.

SERVES 4 AS PART OF A THAI MEAL

4 stalks of lemon grass

6 kaffir lime leaves

6–8 medium red chillies

6 garlic cloves

4–6 Thai shallots or 1–2 regular smallish shallots

4–5 tablespoons *pla raa* (fermented fish sauce)

300g (10½oz) pork, cut in slices

2 tablespoons vegetable oil

about 600ml (20fl oz) water or stock

6 apple aubergines (green apple eggplants) and a handful of pea aubergines (Thai pea eggplants) – maybe 30g (1oz) in all

100g (3½oz) bamboo shoots

300g (10½oz) pumpkin, peeled and cubed – you could also try it with bitter melon (*mara*)

1 large handful of *horapha* (Thai basil)

a large bunch of fresh dill, cut into 5cm (2 inch) pieces

a dash of *nam pla* (fish sauce) or *pla raa* (fermented fish sauce), to taste

Remove the outer sheath from the lemon grass and give it a good bash. Chop it up small, then smash it in a pestle and mortar. Add 1 of the lime leaves, thinly sliced, and the chillies and bash again. Add the garlic and shallots and bash some more. Or do it all in a chopper.

Add the *pla raa* to the paste, then work it into the pork slices. Leave for an hour.

Heat the vegetable oil and fry the meat and paste until cooked and fragrant. Add the water or stock and bring to a simmer. Add the vegetables and cook until just done. Stir in the herbs and a dash more water if you like, and add *nam pla* or *pla raa* to taste. Serve with rice.

CRYING TIGERS, FLYING ANTS AND A SNAKE CALLED SID

ADVENTURES OF A TERRIBLY GREEDY GIRL

Won't Bake, Don't Ask Me...

A few months ago, I took to Twitter to ask:

"What **is** this obsession with cake?"

That's all I wrote.

And suddenly, my feed was alight with comments. I am not alone, it seems.

We need to talk about this because I cannot begin to tell you how irritating it is to read a paragraph that begins "We all love a cake..." I don't.

Don't get me wrong. I can appreciate a gorgeous, thin slice of Sacher Torte at the end of a great meal or with a deep, dark cup of coffee, or a lovely lemon drizzle cake or Victoria sandwich at a picnic on a summer's day. But, seriously, we need to get a grip.

The whole "treat yourself", "naughty indulgence", "cupcake" crap – what are we? Five years old?

I. Just. Don't. Get. It.

Cake is not for breakfast. It is not for lunch. It is not for dinner. It is for tea. Alongside cucumber and egg and cress sandwiches. Or scones.

Can we please change the record? Until we do, I won't bake. So don't ask me.

ADVENTURES OF A TERRIBLY GREEDY GIRL

And Another Thing... 2

Competitive tweeting. You know, when the tweeter has to make sure the tweetee and everyone else on Twitter know they:

1. Have eaten it first

2. Have done it first

3. Were invited, even though they can't attend so and so's event

4. Are more popular/successful/wittier/prettier, all wrapped up in a humble-brag that is a lot more brag than humble.

   You know who you are, Competitive Tweeters. I'm on to you.

ADVENTURES OF A TERRIBLY GREEDY GIRL

No Slices, Whole Pies Only

(or How Brooklyn kept me sane)

I didn't love Manhattan. I know, I know – half of New York will want to slaughter me for writing that, but hear me out. For my first few months in New York, I lived in a friend's apartment in Tribeca. On the 49th floor. At first it seemed amazing – this was *New York*, after all. But little by little, it became isolating. My view was the World Trade Center, which looked great from afar but, up close, was just a very big slab of metal and glass. I never saw my neighbours. The wait for the elevator, the journey *in* the elevator, all alone, was lonely. It wasn't home.

I couldn't put my finger on it, but this wasn't my kind of town. Nora Ephron said she knew she was born to live in New York and everything in between was just preparation. I think of New York City as a learning curve on my way to somewhere else.

And then I discovered Brooklyn. I came across it on a whim. I apartment-sat for a friend in a studio so small you had to back into the toilet to sit on the seat. But I fell in love with the area. This is long before Brooklyn was hip. It was still The Neighbourhood. Atlantic Avenue was packed with Middle Eastern shops selling spices, oils and olive-oil soaps. There was a guy on Court Street who sold essential oils wholesale. It was leafy and fresh, and I wanted in. I stalked into the local realtor and demanded an apartment. Preferably on THAT street, pointing to the most verdant, just across the way.

It turned out that I was in luck. The woman who was walking out as I was walking in had just listed her apartment. And it was on THAT street, just across the way. Within one hour, I had let it, right there, on Wykoff Street. It was beautiful, the basement of a brownstone in Cobble Hill. It looked and felt to me exactly how I thought New York should. If it was 1950. The eat-in kitchen had high tin ceilings, and the bathroom was huge (well, bigger than most – I could at least spread my arms without hitting the wall). There were people sitting on stoops sipping tea or beer. I had NEIGHBOURS that I actually spoke to. And who SPOKE BACK (take that, Tribeca!). They cooked, and the smells wafted into my kitchen through the open back door. I didn't feel I needed to be armed to take an evening stroll. I walked across magnificent Brooklyn Bridge on my way to work and got fit. I discovered my own taste and style – which often meant midnight skip raids and getting lifts home with the Sally Army truck because I couldn't carry my goodies on my own.

The other bonus was that, because Brooklyn was not yet "so hot right now", hardly any models and certainly no colleagues ever came to visit. Weekends were blissfully fashion-free.

The restaurants were local and fabulous. There were the Middle Eastern places on Atlantic, and the fabulous Siam Garden on Court. This was a boon because there weren't so many Thai restaurants in New York back then, so the owners and I became good friends.

But my favourite Brooklyn restaurant will always be Sam's.

Sam's Chop House was run by Brooklyn Lou and his dad. It was an old-school, neighbourhood Italian place with faded booths and red-chequered tablecloths, and a sign in the window which said "No Slices, Whole Pies Only" as though it was a badge of pride. It was as quintessentially New York as you could dream of. The only way to make it more so would have been to put Scorsese and De Niro in one of the booths and make them sing "New York, New York". Lou poured rough but somehow perfect red wine from giant bottles. His dad – the slowest-moving waiter in the world – served huge pizzas and garlicky linguine vongole "with the white sauce" ("Good choice, English, good choice..." – they both always called me "English"), and great characters filled the faded booths.

And you'd hear things like this:

                    LOU
          (to an OLD COUPLE in a booth)
     How ya doin'?

                    OLD MAN
     Not bad, not bad...
          (a beat)
     Hey, you seen the price o' Yankees
     tickets?

174

<pre>
                    LOU
    Right?

                  OLD MAN
    Di Maggio would roll in his grave!
</pre>

Or:

<pre>
                LARGE IRISH GUY
            (to a crowd of mates, all
            tucking into loads of pizza)
        Know what this was called in my house when
        I was a kid? It was called "get that
        foreign shit outta my house!"
</pre>

I spent many an evening sitting in my booth, rough wine in one hand, a pen in the other, dreaming of the sitcom I would write...

Brooklyn restored my sanity. It made me stay in New York longer than I would have. I learned the difference between red and white sauce for linguine vongole. I discovered that you could dial 1-800-MATTRESS and you would have a bed within 12 hours.

I discovered I could be happy anywhere.

NO SLICES, WHOLE PIES ONLY

Linguine alle Vongole

Linguine with clams

I first had this dish in New York cooked by Fran, one of my colleagues at the agency, a second-generation Italian-American whose parents came from Puglia. Frank Forbes, one of the chaps we repped, dug us some clams on Long Island, drove them into the city and brought them to Fran's. She cooked, we drank wine and listened to the soundtrack from *Big Night*. And for one night only, we were transported from Manhattan to Brindisi. It remains pretty much my favourite thing to do to pasta.

SERVES 4

800g (1lb 12oz) fresh clams	12–16 cherry tomatoes (optional)
400g (14oz) linguine	150ml (5fl oz) white wine
2 tablespoons olive oil, plus extra to drizzle	a handful of fresh parsley, finely chopped
3 garlic cloves, finely sliced	sea salt and freshly ground black pepper
2 mild red chillies, finely sliced	

First rinse the clams, discarding any which don't close up when you tap them.

For the pasta, bring a large pan of well-salted water to a rolling boil. Cook the linguine as per the instructions on the packet, until it's *al dente*.

For the clams, heat a sauté pan with a lid over a medium heat and add the olive oil. When it's hot, add the garlic and the chillies, and the tomatoes if you're using them. Stir and cook until the garlic is golden and fragrant, then add the clams and the white wine. Cover the pan and cook, shaking from time to time, until all the clams have opened up. It should take about 5 minutes. Season the sauce with salt and pepper, to taste, then add the parsley and stir it all together.

Drain the pasta when it's cooked and toss it through the sauce. Drizzle with a little extra virgin olive oil, and serve at once.

176

TIP: Remember that the clam juices will already be a little salty, so make sure you taste the sauce before you season it.

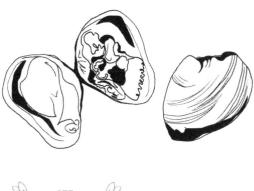

ADVENTURES OF A TERRIBLY GREEDY GIRL

The Comfort of a Roast Chicken

Food writers often reference Proust. I'm not sure how many of us have actually read him – he didn't write any hard-boiled, blood-soaked murder mysteries, which explains why I haven't... that, and the major novel comes in SEVEN VOLUMES (which must have caused him a severe case of carpal tunnel syndrome) – but we've all been at the Cliffs Notes: we all know that just one taste of a petite madeleine dipped in tea sparks the entirety of *À la Recherche du Temps Perdu*. It is the *sine qua non* description for the way in which taste and smell can transport us to another place, another time.

But what if seven volumes could be boiled down to a single beat that captured the evocation, comfort and joy of not just a good dish, but the right dish served at just the right time?

Harold Pinter famously wrote a screenplay of the book – all seven volumes – for Joseph Losey, but they never made the movie because they couldn't put the cash together, so we'll never know if they could have achieved it. The glorious *Babette's Feast* takes a whole film to tenderly reveal the healing power of great food. But for that one moment, we must turn to *Ratatouille*. As fearsome food critic Anton Ego takes his first bite of Remy the Rat's ratatouille, we and he are whisked back to his five-year-old self as his mother comforts him with a bowl of his favourite. Ratatouille. In just three seconds, Brad Bird and his animators engage our empathy and reveal the full emotional clout of food.

I often think of that look on Anton Ego's face. You don't see it often in real life. But when you do, it reminds you of what comfort really means. In the sense of food, it's not simply that something tastes delicious or warming, or that it makes you feel pleasantly full. It's more than that. True comfort food connects you to the hearth, that traditional place at the heart of every home. It gives in every mouthful a mother's embrace. It makes you feel safe.

Comfort food is not about greed or satiation. That's what cravings are for. With an honest, respectable food craving, we're scratching an itch. I know that when I want *sator* (evil Thai stink beans which taste divinely nutty but smell like something the cat dragged in), it's a craving. With fish and chips, it's a craving that's chasing an image – the idea of sitting on a Kentish seafront with my grandparents eating out of newspaper, the smell of vinegar and briny ocean in my nose. A memory I want.

179

With comfort, as ever, I am torn between two things.

On the one hand, there's *pad krapow*. At first glance, this is a deceptively simple dish. A one-plate meal. It's meat (or mushroom or tofu), preferably pork or duck, stir-fried with garlic, chilli, soy and holy basil. With rice. And, ideally, a deep-fried egg on top.

From a pure "mouth" perspective, the three elements – the garlic-basil fire of the stir-fry, the neutral rice, the creamy egg – work together to make a harmony of textures and fragrance that requires a redefinition of the word "perfection". But let's break it down. From top to bottom. The egg.

Where do you start with the egg? What we're discussing here is, essentially, a poached egg... in hot oil. It's the same principle. We want that egg to bubble, protecting that silken runny yolk in a lattice of crisp-to-giving white so that its yellow-red pleasure oooooooooozes over the stir-fry...

... which brings all that garlic fragrance. We all know that the smell of garlic is the smell of good times. The Thai bird's-eyes aren't necessarily the fruitiest chillies, but they bring the heat in a round, fat, middle-of-the-tongue burn that makes the mouth water. The meat brings that slightly caramelized umami – if you have the right kind of fire, you can achieve enough hints of the Maillard reaction to *satisfy* (and when I italicize "satisfy", it's to make you understand that I mean it in a soul singer kind of a way). The holy basil provides a punch of anise to startle the most jaded.

And then there's the rice. How can I explain to you the meaning of rice? Rice is not meant to be smothered. It doesn't exist to sop up your curry. Rice is the star. Haing Ngor, the much missed, kind, delightful, Oscar-winning star of *The Killing Fields*, wrote so evocatively about the role of rice in his memoir, *Survival in the Killing Fields* (originally *A Cambodian Odyssey* in the US): "Under the Khmer Rouge, we hardly ever ate rice – not rice as it should be, with each grain separate and moist, and a clean, fragrant steam rising from the bowl... Rice is the centre of our meals, a clean, neutral medium that sets off the flavours of the other food we add to it." Boy, does it ever.

For Thais, too, rice is everything. If you want to ask someone if they've had their lunch or dinner, you ask: *kin khao ayung?* Literally, it translates as "Have you eaten rice yet?" With *hom mali*, jasmine rice, the smell alone is home.

ADVENTURES OF A TERRIBLY GREEDY GIRL

It's the hearth.

A friend of mine, with an Italian heritage, once told me that, whenever he moved to somewhere new, the first thing he did was cook tomato sauce. To him, it made the place smell like home. Thai rice does something similar to me. But if I'm searching for the ultimate comfort, I don't make *pad krapow*.

I roast a chicken. It's the dish I come home to. Since school, since work, since forever.

The thing about roast chicken is that it's not a restaurant dish. No chicken "out" can ever match a chicken at home, just out of the oven, its skin brown, brittle perfection, its flesh yielding and delicious. No one else can make the gravy the way *you* make it. A roast chicken is deeply personal, all cheffy tricks aside. If it's a dish that matters to you, and I suspect it does to many, you learn by smell and touch how to make it... just so.

One of my food heroes, Khun Toi, runs a chicken stand in Chiang Dao. He'll never tell me the secret to his recipe (we've discussed this), but a part of his genius is that he knows how people like their chicken. Thais, for example, generally prefer theirs drier than *farangs*. We want it moist. Khun Toi knows how to make sure (until he sells out) that everyone gets what they want.

The same is true of a roast. I want my chicken perfumed with lemon and herbs and garlic. Sometimes I want to roast the potatoes beside it, so they absorb the chicken fat and butter. Sometimes I want them separate. Always, I want greens. Cavolo nero, if possible, but I'm not picky. And always gravy. These days, it's usually some kind of wine reduction. But, back in the day, I'd make it with the vegetable water, cooking it down with the roasting residue into a glorious harmony that was really an exaggeration of the flavours on my plate.

Roast chicken reminds me of my Mum. It reminds me of coming home from school to Thailand and telling her my news – all the stuff you couldn't put in a letter, but wanted to tell because it was funny or sad or impossible.

Roast chicken reminds me of the home that bore me. Of the hearth. Of that ancient idea of a female goddess of the life-giving fire.

Roast chicken reminds me of why we are alive.

And that, my friends, is comfort food.

THE COMFORT OF A ROAST CHICKEN

My Perfect Roast Chicken

SERVES 4

1 × 1.5kg (3lb 5oz) chicken

6 garlic cloves, chopped roughly, plus 2 bulbs of garlic, left unpeeled and halved

150ml (5fl oz) chicken stock

150ml (5fl oz) white wine

a bunch of fresh thyme

a handful of fresh flat-leaf parsley

1 small onion, halved

1 lemon, halved, plus lemon juice, to taste

unsalted butter

olive oil

sea salt and freshly ground black pepper

Preheat the oven to 200°C (400°F), Gas Mark 6.

Place the chicken in a skillet or roasting pan that is just big enough to hold it. Trim out any excess fat in the cavity and discard. Season the cavity with salt and pepper. Then pop in the garlic cloves, thyme, parsley and onion. Squeeze both the lemon halves over the chicken and stuff one half inside the bird. Finish with a knob of good unsalted butter.

Drizzle some good olive oil all over the bird and season well with salt and pepper. Place another knob of butter in the creases between the legs and the body and pop a piece on the breast as well.

Roast in the oven for 1½ hours, basting every 20 minutes. 40 minutes before the end of cooking, throw in the halved bulbs of garlic and give them a shake to coat them in the buttery juices.

Check the chicken is done by piercing the fattest part of the leg and thigh with a skewer or knife. If the juices are running clear, it's done. If not, pop back in for 10–15 more minutes.

Remove the herbs from inside the cavity into the pan and remove the chicken from the pan, along with the garlic bulbs. Pop on a plate and rest in a warm place for 10–15 minutes before serving.

Meanwhile place the skillet or roasting tin on a medium heat. Add the stock and wine and bring to a simmer, scraping up any roasting residues from the bottom of the pan. Reduce by at least a third, if not more, then season with salt, pepper and lemon juice to taste. Finally, finish with a knob of cold butter to render your gravy silky.

Serve with crispy roast potatoes and greens, or a bitter leaf salad.

Remember to save the bones to make a stock. For soup. For risotto. For its sheer chicken-y goodness.

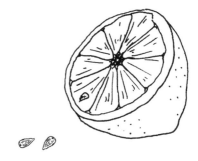

THE COMFORT OF A ROAST CHICKEN

ADVENTURES OF A TERRIBLY GREEDY GIRL

Diet is a Four-Letter Word

By the age of 16, chubby (and not in a cheery way) with a tight curly perm and specs, I had probably been on every diet in the book. I'd done the Beverly Hills – pineapple, pineapple and more pineapple: heartburn and a lifelong hatred of pineapple; the Cabbage Soup: excessive wind; the Mayo Clinic: bad breath and constipation; SlimFast: fainting, extreme hunger, spots and a filthy temper. I could recite calorie contents the way others could recite the Kings and Queens of England. It was... Not... Good.

I dieted constantly from my early teens until I was 30 and was dumped by fax by a man who'd written a film called *Halibut* (don't ask – as far as I know, it was never made). While I was on a business trip. To Thailand.

Classy.

I was at my lowest. Being dumped always made me think about my weight. So I decided to go guerrilla and put myself through some Hardcore Weight Loss, dragging my friend Jan to a place on Koh Samui where we would be *compelled* to fast for ten whole days. More than fast. There were daily colema treatments. For the uninitiated, this involves a slanted board with a hole in the middle. Carefully place the board over the toilet. Lie down on said board with your cheeks positioned above the hole. Insert a tube into your bum. Then pass 5 litres of kaolin-infused water into your colon. By yourself. So you can cut the flow off at any time. It is an extremely sophisticated contraption with a clothes peg as the off switch.

We were supposed to do this until we were drained – literally and psychologically.

It was tedious, too. Jan, to her enduring credit, managed both to read and smoke on her slant board. (Skills.) Me, not so much. I found that you needed to be "hands on" with that clothes peg. (Accidents.)

Our slant boards came with a sieve. And we were encouraged by the staff to look, with chopsticks, at what it caught. I heard tales of crayons, marbles and small toys which had allegedly been buried in the mass of old filth and tar-like rot in people's guts for decades. One woman swore she had retrieved a small animal, but I never saw evidence of it. All I had was a putrid mass, followed by a strange amber jelly once my system was devoid of discernible food. We would then have group discussions about our findings.

Our group consisted of Jan and I, a couple who made opium pipes and a man who sold double-glazing in Nepal. Which was enterprising, when you think about it.

Their scintillating company notwithstanding, our real problem was that our room was right above a very good restaurant. As we lay in bed each night, stomachs grumbling, deep in the gin withdrawal, the smells of basil fried rice and fresh grilled fish would waft into our room. It was cruel. Very cruel.

And so we ran away – two 30-year-old women, giggling like schoolgirls, delirious with starvation – all the way to the nearest town for a tattoo and a bowl of *khao tom*, or rice porridge. Each mouthful was bliss. Silky smooth grains of jasmine rice, fragrant broth and minced pork, with pickled turnip and deep-fried garlic. The pleasure far outweighed the guilt.

We finished our meal, paid and... then I had to use the loo. Right, now you're picturing the sort of toilet you're used to. But this was rural Thailand, so we're talking about a squatty. A Thai squatty is not like an old-fashioned European squatty. It comes with a hose to wash your nethers clean when you're done, and a large bucket of clean water with a scoop to flush it manually. You have to learn, from an early age, how to balance just so, so that you don't pee all over your feet. I hoicked up my skirt, pulled down my pants, looked into the pan to take aim... and came face to face with a massive rat, its fierce incisors mere inches from my bum.

I can't speak for the rat. I imagine it looked surprised. I screamed, and burst from the bathroom, knickers akimbo, shouting "*Noo yai! Noo yai!*" ("Rat! Rat!"), crashing through a newly laid-up table and clattering to the floor. There's embarrassment. And then there's accidentally flashing a full restaurant post a run-in with a rat.

Karma is a bitch.

To paraphrase Jack Crabbe in the glorious *Little Big Man*, "That was the end of my dieting days."

Still, it makes me wonder: where did this insatiable need to be thin come from? How did this idea of being "the right weight" – whatever that is – get in my head?

I have asked myself over and over. When did it start? It didn't stem from the

ADVENTURES OF A TERRIBLY GREEDY GIRL

fashion biz. I never compared myself to models. They are another species. For 5-foot, 1-inch me to compare myself to these gazelles would be like comparing a fish to a bird.

No, it was definitely earlier.

I was always chubby. Which is not surprising, for I was a very greedy child, hobbit-like in my penchant for first, second and even third breakfasts – one inside for *farang* or Anglo food, then one or two outside for Thai. I had my cheeks pinched by everyone as they uttered *"Gam jui"* ("sweet cheeks") so hard I had permanent bruises. My nanny and her friends loved my little white rolls of fat. So there was nothing there to create such a negative self-image.

No. It came from closer to home.

It came from my mother, who was on a constant diet for as long as I can remember, and from my sister, who obsessed about her weight and still has the capacity, through no fault of her own, to make me feel

a. Like a whale

b. Outrageously greedy

and remains very, very slim. But she works at it. And quite frankly, my dears, I don't.

And it came from a cold and draughty English boarding school, where they weighed and measured us in the sports hall in front of our class mates. My cheeks would burn with shame if I had put on weight over the holidays. And more often than not, I had. It came from Grandad Plunkett telling me I was fat all the time. It came from a boy – nay, a young man – telling me that he might consider dating me if I lost 10 pounds. And it's *this* feeling that lasted.

No matter how old I got and how much I talked myself into seeing sense and just "being", I couldn't help but have pangs of guilt. When I ate with both Kim and Mum, my insecurity kicked in. Yet, even as they shared a starter, I would furiously order two. Because, fuck it. And eat it all, eyes stinging with shame. In practically all the telephone conversations I remember with dear Mum, her opening gambit was, "So... how's your weight?"

 187

It did not start with her. Oh no. There was family form for this. Gran would always have a go at Mum about her weight, too. My uncle's favourite saying is "an inch to the lips, an inch to the hips". It was a constant growing up. It is conditioning. Even as recently as last year, before he died, Dad said to me, "You've never been slim, have you? You are shaped like your mother. Round."

But… finally… I think I might be there. Maybe it's the loss of my parents; maybe it's entering my fifties and no longer giving a damn what people think of me or, more importantly, what I PERCEIVE they think of me. I have accepted that this curvy body leans towards a UK size 12. I have thrown out all the size 8 dresses and tops that I would torture myself for not being able to squeeze into. My skin looks fabulous – the fat is like a cheap form of filler. I understand that there comes a point in a woman's life when she has to make a choice about which she prefers to look good: her face or her arse, and I am comfortable in Team Face. I eat what I want – not to excess. I five-two. I drink the occasional glass of my liver-flush elixir (see overleaf) when I have over-indulged on the martinis. I take long walks with the blessing that is wee Maya the dog. My husband loves me. My blood pressure is stable. I have a banging cleavage. I am happy.

So, take that, DIET, you foolish four-letter word. It took me 40 years, but you lose.

189

DIET IS A FOUR-LETTER WORD

Liver Flush Drink

Oh dear. Here it is. The infamous Liver Flush.

It is by no means delicious but, if you're on some sort of health kick and have knocked the booze on the head for a bit – give it a go. You may even feel your liver contract.

MAKES 1 LARGE NOXIOUS DRINK

2 tablespoons extra virgin olive oil

150ml (5fl oz) lemon or lime juice

5 garlic cloves

4cm (1½ inch) piece of fresh root ginger, peeled and chopped

½–1 teaspoon cayenne pepper

a splash of orange juice to sweeten, if you like

Whack all the ingredients through a blender or juicer, and drink before beginning a diet or fast. Wait. And feel the burn.

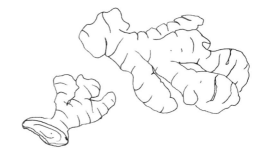

DIET IS A FOUR-LETTER WORD

ADVENTURES OF A TERRIBLY GREEDY GIRL

Is That How You Do It?

(or How to avoid divorce over dinner)

When I first met my husband I was furious. He had asked me out so many times; I had put him off so many times. But, like a bird after a worm, he persisted. Finally, I relented. I had no more energy for excuses. So it was to be 7pm sharp. My club. A quick drink. Done. I could probably even charge it to expenses.

As one would for a date, I dressed myself meticulously that day. I wore a shocking-pink Lilly Pulitzer top, a red Fair Isle cardigan, a black and white A-line DVF skirt and rather ugly, chunky silver sandals, with tights. No make-up. Unkempt hair. If this didn't put him off, then he was a weirdo.

7pm precisely. I am there in a booth with a martini. He walks in. Tells me I look lovely. Orders a drink. One martini turns into five. Before I know it we are leaning against a lamppost outside Fortnum's (keeping it classy), getting familiar with each other's tonsils.

I am smitten. Damn.

The second date was at his house. (Yes, I know: how brave of me.) For dinner. I half expected a pizza or, at best, some sort of ready meal. But uh, no. Here was *coq au vin* made with guinea fowl, crisp green beans and silken mashed potatoes. A bottle of Chateau Musar red. Damn again. He nailed it. I was beginning to think: maybe he's a keeper.

In return, I cooked for him some nights later. And here was the ultimate test. Thai food. If he didn't like it, well, that would be that, good cook or no. Not just any Thai food. I reached for the big gun. *Nam prik kapi*. A fermented shrimp paste, lime and chilli dip that is... pungent, to say the least. I waited, I watched. If he could handle that... He ate the lot. All of it. Smacked his lips and asked what else was on the menu. Done deal. We were inseparable from that moment on.

Friends of his started to warn me with subtle hints. He was a back-seat cook. He was territorial about his kitchen. He could be an ogre at the oven. Remember, we were in the throes of that first rush of hormones: even pepper-grinding was sexy, so I saw none of these traits. Until one day he asked me, as I was making something I had made a hundred times and, bearing in mind I am eight years older than him, had been making well before he had: "Is that how

193

YOU do it?" The steam started pouring out of my ears, yes, those same ears that remained deaf to the warnings. He claims he was asking out of pure curiosity. From his tone, I was braced for man-splaining and was ready to argue back.

And so it began. The negotiation. Would we be able to cook together in the same kitchen or head for certain divorce? To deal with this question I have, over time, instigated a few rules:

1. Make sure you have your roles straight. He doesn't do Thai food – unless under strict instructions from me. I don't interfere with his coq au vin. Job done.

2. He makes the drinks. And the dessert. Unless it's ice cream, in which case I do it.

3. He must never, ever try to make pastry. Especially in front of children. Their parents would never forgive us for the language they'd learn.

4. When entertaining, one is in the kitchen, the other actually entertaining. Tag-team it so that each of you gets a break from the stove.

5. Always wash up the glasses the next day.

6. Coarse sea salt. Not Maldon flakes.

7. There will always be a stash of dried shrimp, squid and horse mackerel crowding out the fridge and a growing number of shrimp-paste brands. Get used to it.

8. Always have gin and wine in the house. Always.

9. Keep the knives sharp. If I *have* to kill him, this will make it easier.

ADVENTURES OF A TERRIBLY GREEDY GIRL

Surprisingly, this has worked. We cook differently. And that's okay. I have someone on hand who'll cook through my recipes when I've finished writing them. (He calls it "idiot testing" – if he can follow it, he says, then anyone can...) And if there's even a hint of "Is that how you do it/are going to do it?", I make like Paddington: I give him my hardest stare. Then I pass him something and say, "Chop that, and pour me a glass of wine."

Oscars Rabbit

(or Braised rabbit with garlic and fennel)

I'd love to be able to tell you that this recipe came from a wizened and brilliant French cook whom I met in a tiny restaurant in an unfashionable corner of Provence, known only to very few. But you'd know at once that I was lying because Provence no longer has any unfashionable corners.

The truth is, Fred and I first made this in LA on Oscars Sunday several years ago, after I'd found some stunning fennel in Hollywood Farmers' Market that morning. I can't remember why, exactly, I decided to cook it with rabbit. But, whatever the reason, we dashed down Sunset to Peking Poultry in Chinatown for a rabbit so fresh it was still warm and aquiver. It proved the ideal thing to cook for a couple in the kitchen, because one of us could focus on the rabbit, the other on the fennel, and thus conflict could be avoided.

I think the whole French vibe was kicked off by the fact that Marion Cotillard was up for best actress for *La Vie en Rose*. Or it could have been because the light in Los Angeles always slightly reminds me of Provence. Either way, it all went very well with a Provençal rosé (for the cooking phase) and a delicious Rhône-style Californian red from the beloved Silverlake Wine.

Herbsaint, should you be able to find it, is a take on *pastis* from the fair city of New Orleans. If anything, it has a slightly more pronounced aniseed flavour than *pastis*, but it doesn't turn cloudy when you dilute it.

SERVES 4

For the rabbit:

2 tablespoons olive oil

1 rabbit (about 1.5 kg/3lb 5oz), jointed, with liver and kidneys

40ml (1½fl oz) Herbsaint or pastis

4–6 whole garlic cloves, crushed in their skins

1 tablespoon picked thyme leaves

1 bay leaf

125ml (4fl oz) white wine

125ml (4fl oz) water

25g (1oz) butter

sea salt and freshly ground black pepper

1 tablespoon freshly chopped parsley, to garnish

For the fennel:

25g (1oz) unsalted butter

1 tablespoon olive oil

2 bulbs of fennel, trimmed and quartered

1 tablespoon caster (superfine) sugar

50ml (2fl oz) white wine

Preheat the oven to 180°C (350°F), Gas Mark 4.

First cook the rabbit. Heat the olive oil in a sauté pan with a metal handle. Season the rabbit well, and fry the pieces (including the kidneys; I like to pan-fry the livers in the same pan, and set them aside when they are just pink inside to make crostini) in the olive oil until they are well browned all over. You may have to do this in batches so as not to overcrowd them.

Pop all the pieces back into the pan and flambé with the Herbsaint or pastis.

Add the garlic, thyme, bay leaf and wine. Bring to the boil, then put into the oven uncovered for about 35 minutes or until cooked through.

While the rabbit's in the oven, cook the fennel. Heat the butter and oil in a skillet or frying pan. Add the fennel quarters, sugar and wine and, over a low heat, slowly allow to caramelize until the fennel is golden brown and just tender. Remove from the pan and set aside.

When the rabbit is cooked, remove from its pan and set aside on a warmed platter with the caramelized fennel.

Add the water to the rabbit's pan juices, bubble up and reduce by half. Add the butter, and stir through the sauce until the butter is completely melted and combined.

Pour the sauce over the rabbit and fennel, discard the bay leaf, garnish with the parsley, and serve with crusty bread and a salad.

197

10 Things I Learned from My Elephant

So I have an elephant. I don't own an elephant, *per se*. But (and now I have to think of the best way to put this) we've had a relationship for over 20 years.

When I first met Bo-That, he was probably about five years old and doomed to life as a street elephant until his then owners heard about *Operation Dumbo Drop* and brought him to our production base. There we had several elephants: Tai the movie star, and some that had come up from the Elephant Conservation Centre in Lampang to work as extras. I persuaded the studio to buy Bo-That and to give him to the Lampang Centre, and I did so because life as a street elephant is tough. It was still legal back then, too. Mendicants tour their elephant through the tourist centres, begging and offering rides under dubious circumstances. It's no life for an animal. Especially one as magnificent as this.

Bo-That was named after the lead elephant character in the movie. He was small – a little over 3 feet tall at the shoulder. And he was adorable. It was hard to leave him when the unit moved back to Bangkok to wrap up. But I promised I'd keep in touch.

And so I have: I have sent money for his upkeep, visited whenever I can, argued with the head vet at the Centre about what's best for him. He's now a massive bull tusker, a good 8 feet or more at the shoulder, and about four tons of bone and muscle, my big, beautiful boy.

As you'd expect, elephants have a way about them. Like all animals, they have as much to teach us as we have to teach them, so here are a few things I've picked up along the way.

1. It is absolutely true: elephants never forget. After *Dumbo Drop*, I went straight onto a van Damme flick called *The Quest* in southern Thailand. After it wrapped, I didn't make it back to Thailand for ten years, when I took Fred for his first time. Of course, we went to the Centre in Lampang. It took a little asking around, but we found Bo-That in the elephant stables with his *kwan* (mahout), Tam. He recognized me instantly, reaching out with his trunk to touch my face and all but hug me. Let's say that Tam was quite surprised. Bo-That has a reputation for being *doot* (the "oo"

pronounced like "wood" as opposed to "hoot"). It means fierce. Or thereabouts. It's a tricky word to translate. But he remembered me well. And fondly. Which was the surprise. Bottom line, Bo-That is not really a people elephant. He likes Tam. Thankfully, he likes me. He tolerates everybody else.

2. If an elephant doesn't want to do something, there is no way on earth you can make it. They are sociable creatures, and they will put up with a lot. But if you think that you can make one do your bidding when it doesn't want to... you have another thing coming.

3. If you don't like the person on your back, throw them off. Now. Let me explain... Bo-That has never been the most even-tempered elephant. And when he reached adulthood and went into must, well, he was not very pleasant to be around. As one unlucky tourist found out. For a little while, Bo-That worked as a taxi elephant. But this particular tourist thought it would be a good idea, mid-ride, to make fun of him. So Bo-That threw him off. He never had to be a taxi elephant again...

4. It's important to keep yourself occupied. After the riding incident, above, the Centre decided that perhaps it was not such a good idea to have Bo-That around the tourists. The combination of his *doot*-ness and must made him simply too dangerous. So he was sent off to spend some me-time in the forest. This was not as idyllic as it sounds. It would have been far too dangerous to let him roam, so he had to be chained up. And, while it was a very long chain, it was still a chain. Nor was it ideal for Tam because, with his elephant not working, he couldn't work either. Bo-That was lonely and he was miserable. I pleaded with the vet that there had to be something better for him than living on his own in the forest. And this is where things get difficult: a young bull elephant is a dangerous thing. In the wild, at Bo-That's age, young males band together for company – imagine a gang of 4-ton mods tearing up the forest on their mopeds – before forming their own herds and making baby elephants. But he has never lived in the wild.

10 THINGS I LEARNED FROM MY ELEPHANT

And there isn't a lot of wild left. So his life, for better or worse, has to be managed. Couldn't we, I asked the vet, at the very least, find him something to *do*? The vet said he'd think about it. The next time we saw him, Bo-That had a job. In the legitimate logging business. And he was much happier. In case you're wondering, in Thai law elephants retire at 60.

5. You don't really know your place in the world until you walk beside an elephant. The softness of their footsteps, almost as silent as a cat's, astounds. If something this large can be so gentle, surely we as a species are missing something.

6. Horse flies are bad, but elephant flies are worse. If you have a proboscis that can draw blood on an elephant, you're bad news.

7. Happiness sounds like a deep, contented rumble.

8. Even elephants have their favourite foods. Of the ones I know well, Poongmi (who's cared for by Tam's uncle, and is at the time of writing pregnant) *loovvvveeeeesssss* bamboo. She will do almost anything for it. And if you're on her back when she sees a good patch of it in the forest, you'd better hang on tight. Salawin, the gentlest soul you could imagine, is obsessed with bananas. Bo-That's bliss is a large sticky tamarind ball, especially in hot weather.

9. The elephant is the ultimate all-terrain vehicle. The only surface they can't handle is hot tarmac. It burns their feet.

10. A lot of people object to the very idea of elephants in captivity, of working elephants, of riding elephants. It's something I think about a lot. My head tells me that Bo-That is in the best place he can be. My heart often disagrees because I worry about him. Bo-That is a massive, magnificent bull tusker. And he is dangerous. In the wild, he would almost certainly have been shot by now, if not for his tusks then for rampaging around. In

ADVENTURES OF A TERRIBLY GREEDY GIRL

captivity, all that raw maleness doesn't make him any safer. I have asked the vets if we can mate him, if only to burn some of it out of him. They worry that he would become so over-excited he would harm the female, and I have to trust their judgement. So he is kept busy with work so he doesn't get bored. He burns off energy, and socializes with other elephants, which is profoundly important. Horsey friends tell me that working with stallions is not dissimilar. Like Bo-That, they want to run free and be their own boss. All that untrammelled testosterone coursing through a domesticated beast — it has to go somewhere. (I worked with male models... believe me... I know...) When I make the connection of horses to elephants, I do so knowing that humans have worked with both species for a very long time. And, with both species, there is good practice and there is bad. I have seen wonderful horsemen and women and I've seen bad, just as I have with *kwans*. Believe me, I want as many elephants to survive in the wild as possible. But I also know that all our good intentions — preserving habitat, training rangers, all that — will too often be trumped by other people's greed. We live in an increasingly managed natural world. It seems to me that, for its species's survival, the domesticated elephant is not too high a price to pay.

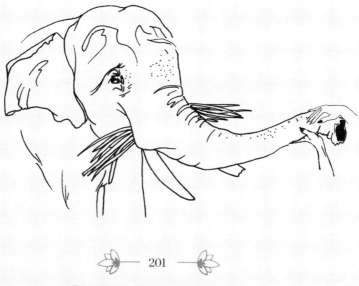

10 THINGS I LEARNED FROM MY ELEPHANT

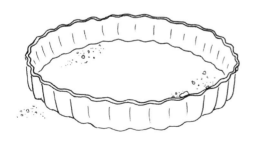

ADVENTURES OF A TERRIBLY GREEDY GIRL

Life, Death and Steak 'n' Kidney Pie

They wheeled out a trolley covered in tattered, stained sheets which the attendant plucked off with a practised flourish. She wore mismatched clothes. A summer skirt with a novelty sweater and open-toed sandals. It was January, for God's sake. Her arms were stiffly crossed over her chest in a poor imitation of piety. Her skin was grey and waxen, her eyes blue pools staring into nothing. The family gathered to drop warm tears onto her cold cheeks. All except me.

It was the last time I saw my mother.

I hadn't wanted to see her body. I'd wanted to remember her the way she was when I'd seen her last. But Dad, broken and bereft, had insisted and I didn't know how, in that moment, with so many emotions zipping hither and thither like gnats on a river evening, to do what I felt was right for me. So I went in.

Maybe it's a generational thing. Dad always wanted to visit a body before it was buried. When Gran died, and Mum was too sick to travel to the Isle of Man for the funeral, he had asked me if he should take a picture of Gran's body so he could show it to her. "No!" I said, shocked at what I saw as morbidity. But to him, it was a last goodbye.

To me, standing in that awful room, there was no one here to say goodbye to. Mum was gone, and all that remained was a husk dressed in an outfit that, excuse me, she wouldn't be seen dead in. Another reason I knew she was gone.

I tend to save my grief for later. And I tend to find myself helping others through the worst of it, knowing I'll take my turn in private when I know they're done.

But that night, I needed something to take that awful image of Mum's body from my eyes. I needed to conjure her, my way, to say the goodbye that Dad had said that afternoon.

I made her steak and kidney pie.

Relatives sat around with red-rimmed eyes and large glasses of wine, looking dazed. Dad was like a man who had lost something he'd assumed would always be there.

They needed to be fed. This was the first thing, the only thing, that came into my mind. I didn't have a recipe – Mum hardly ever wrote anything down. I just

cooked it. It was almost as if she were there, guiding me. It was perfect – just like hers. We were quiet, all eating, all consumed by memories. *Good* memories, with a few smiles, because that's what good food does. It's evocative and healing. It shows love and kindness. It is life-affirming. I have come to think that the connection between cooking and death is as solid as that between sex and death. It's just that cooking a meal is a lot more of a group activity.

Something similar happened when Dad died. Again, it was the night before the funeral – always a tough, uncomfortable time, when you are dreading and yet longing for the next day to be done. I thought we could celebrate Dad's life by eating all his favourite dishes. I made Thai fish cakes, green curry, pork belly and ginger curry, a *som tam* and of course steamed jasmine rice. He loved the smell of rice. And again, we started to smile and tell tales, and reminisce about those long-ago Thai days, fishing off the beach or telling dirty jokes, barbecuing and boating.

When someone dies, it is always hard to find the right words of comfort, even within families. We may have lost the same person, but that loss is unique to each of us, just as each of our relationships is uniquely ours. And when a parent dies, it is not just the person who is gone, but a slice of a collective memory too. For none of us remembers everything. We rely on each other in a family to fill in the stories so that, together, we remember more. When we write things down, we preserve them. And though the things not written down seem often more alive – they evolve in each telling as new memories are added or older ones embellished into something funnier or sadder – in the storyteller's death, we lose them altogether. Gone now are the memories of my mother as a girl, of my father's evacuation from South London in the war. Gone too are the stories of the culture shock that shaped them, from Lewisham to Bangkok before the '60s had even swung. I will never hear those tales again. But I will cook this pie. It is my act of remembrance.

LIFE, DEATH AND STEAK 'N' KIDNEY PIE

Betty's Steak and Kidney Pie

My mother Betty had big blue eyes, cool pastry hands and dangerous curves. This pie is as much hers as I can make it.

SERVES 4–6

750g (1lb 10oz) braising steak – I like chuck – sliced into strips

250g (9oz) lamb's kidneys, cleaned, cored and cut into small pieces

2 tablespoons seasoned flour, plus extra flour, for dusting

2 tablespoons vegetable oil

1 large onion, finely chopped

1 garlic clove, finely chopped

650ml (22fl oz) Oxo stock (or other beef stock)

a good few dashes of Worcestershire sauce

a dash of Angostura bitters

a dash of anchovy essence (optional)

a few sprigs of fresh thyme, leaves only (optional)

sea salt and freshly ground black pepper

For the pastry:

200g (7oz) plain (all-purpose) flour

100g (3½oz) butter, or 50g (1¾oz) butter and 50g (1¾oz) lard/margarine – cold from the fridge

iced water, as needed

1 egg, beaten, to glaze

You will also need a pie dish or baking dish.

Toss the steak and the kidney pieces into the seasoned flour, shaking off any excess, and set aside.

Heat the oil in a heavy-based casserole. Once hot, fry the beef until lightly browned all over. You will need to do this in batches. Remove and set aside. Now add the kidneys and toss until brown. Remove and set aside with the beef.

ADVENTURES OF A TERRIBLY GREEDY GIRL

Add a little more oil if you like at this point. Add the onions and stir over a low heat until they have started to soften. Add the garlic and cook a little longer. Put the beef and kidneys and any accrued juices back into the casserole and add the stock. Add Worcestershire sauce, Angostura bitters, and the anchovy essence and thyme if using. Bring to the boil, then turn down the heat, cover and simmer VERY gently for 1½–2 hours, until very tender and the gravy has thickened. Alternatively, pop it into a low oven (160°C/325°F/Gas Mark 3) for 1½–2 hours.

Remove from the heat or oven and taste. Adjust the seasoning accordingly. Then allow to cool completely.

To make the pastry, rub together the flour and the butter or butter and lard/margarine mixture until you get the texture of fine breadcrumbs. Add a pinch of salt. Add some iced water a little at a time until the pastry starts coming together – be careful not to add too much or your pastry will be tough. We want light, buttery, melt-in-the-mouth pastry. Gather it gently into a ball, wrap well in cling film (plastic wrap) and pop it into the fridge for about 30 minutes.

Heat the oven to 200°C (400°F), Gas Mark 6.

Flour a large enough surface well. Gently start rolling the pastry out to fit your pie dish, with a little overlap.

Pour the filling into the dish or tin – make sure it sits at the rim or even a bit above: we don't want the pastry sinking. Wet the rim of the dish and place the pastry carefully over the pie. Seal the edges gently.

Brush the beaten egg all over the pastry. Make a small hole in the middle of the lid to allow steam to escape. If you have any pastry scraps left, make some little leaves or other decorations – Mum would sometimes put leaves and berries on.

Place in the oven for 35–40 minutes or until crisp and golden on top.

Serve with mashed potatoes, peas and extra gravy.

LIFE, DEATH AND STEAK 'N' KIDNEY PIE

ADVENTURES OF A TERRIBLY GREEDY GIRL

Gin, Sweat and Tears

No one tells you. One day, you are yourself – normal, and going about your business. The next day... BAM! You are suddenly a half-crazed, sweating mess with frizzed hair and constant beads of moisture on your top lip. Your husband thinks you have been possessed. Even the cats skirt around you when you walk into the room. You wake up drenched, with palpitations playing like Gene Krupa on your ribcage, filled with anxiety and portents of doom. Then it dawns on you...

Fuck...

I'm 50.

The word

MENOPAUSE

lights up in neon like an ad in Times Square and dances before your eyes.

I had a book coming out when she reared her ugly head. Three months of sheer and utter panic, every day mentally unpicking my manuscript and finding fault. It didn't matter that everyone told me it was "wonderful"; I could find a million ways that it could send me into a tailspin.

Reverse adolescence is what it is. Without the spots. And, no, you can't run into your room and slam the door and shout, "I hate you." Well, you can. I tried. But it doesn't help. That much.

Then there's the fear that your husband will replace you with a younger, saner model. Then again, that would only mean that he would have to go through this twice. Or more if he traded in again. Depending on how long he lived. And at that point I wasn't sure how long I did want him to live.

Then there are the periods. Or the lack of them. She is a sneaky little bitch, the menopause. Just when you think it's all over. Just when you think it's safe to go back into the figurative water – KABOOM – thar she blows again. And it's a gusher. Like Daniel Day-Lewis in *There Will Be Blood* (oh yes) has just struck oil in your pants, and you haven't bought a tampon in the last three months because you were *just beginning to allow yourself to think you didn't need them any more.*

No warning.

At all.

And since you now feel constantly moody and fat, who's to know if it's the PMS back again or the menopause taunting you?

And how long does this go on for? No one can tell you. Should you try HRT? The side effects could be fatal. And you now have high blood pressure, so that's a no-no anyway. OK. "Do you have ANYTHING?" I ask the doctor. Nope. Oh – and avoid alcohol and spicy food. Like hell is that going to happen. Jesus. Don't take away my gin. Not now.

Then there's that lovely ring of fat that starts to appear round your middle, the disappearing waist. You aren't eating more. Or drinking (much) more. You exercise. You do everything you're supposed to. But. It. Just. Won't. Shift. All your bras are tight. You wonder, "Why are my boobs getting bigger?" I didn't sign on for this!

Spanx enters stage left. Mercilessly, I squeeze myself into a lycra tube which seems only to suck the fat up from one area to deposit it in another. "You canna defy the laws of physics," it says, like a stern, elastic Scotty. When I look in the mirror for the first time, I remind myself of an early-'70s Walls sausage – tubular and fatty-pork pale. I persevere. I do. But sitting at dinners with that type of constriction borders on torture.

The less said about the extra hair you suddenly start sprouting, the better. Oh, and then there's the loss of *other* hair. Turns out there's no need for a bikini wax after 50. Not that this bothers me. I got waxed once. Fred said it reminded him of a skinned cat.

Eventually, this too will end. But, ever since The Gusher, I now own more tampons than Boots and I have them stashed in every bag or winter coat pocket I can think of, just in case I am caught out again. So now I have to wonder: when the time comes, what do I do with the inevitable Tampon Mountain™? I could open them up for the cats to play with, I suppose. Pick-up sticks for felines. They are vaguely mouse-like. Can you donate an open pack? Use them for fire starters? Or eye make-up removal? How much longer will I have to keep buying them?

Now, I'm not the man-blaming type, unless The Man in question really is

ADVENTURES OF A TERRIBLY GREEDY GIRL

to blame (like he is over equal pay...). But I do wonder: if the other half of the world's population had to spend three-quarters of their lives either bleeding or sweating, they'd have come up with a handy little pill to pop by now, surely. I mean, scientists are meant to be inquisitive. When you realize that only three species *on the entire fucking planet* endure the menopause – and the other two are whales – you'd think someone would have enough curiosity to figure it out. Wouldn't you? There's at least a PhD in it. And a regular spot on Radio 4.

In the absence of a proper expert, I have my own solution to the travails of another week in the Clutches of the Bitch. I pay homage to the classic steak dinner as served at Musso and Frank's Grill in Hollywood. If it worked for Bettys Davis and Bacall, it will bloody well work for me:

A Friday Night's Dinner at Musso and Frank's Grill

The Perfect Grilled Steak, Charred and Rare

....

SERVES 2–4
(DEPENDING ON WHETHER YOU SPLIT THEM OR NOT)

2 steaks (I favour a bone-in ribeye)

1 garlic clove, halved

olive oil, to coat

sea salt and freshly ground black pepper

Remove the steaks from the fridge in plenty of time to make sure they come up to room temperature. Then, about half an hour before you plan to cook, rub the steaks on both sides with the garlic (an old Elizabeth David trick), then with olive oil and season liberally with salt and pepper.

If you don't have an outside grill on the go, preheat a cast-iron skillet or griddle until you're worried that you're about to have something akin to a Three Mile Island meltdown on your stove top. Cook on both sides to your satisfaction. I want mine charred and rare. You might prefer yours differently. The only way to test it is by feel – if you press the ball of your thumb, you'll see it goes from soft and squishy above the joint to hard by your wrist. That soft and squishy feeling is what a rare steak feels like. The closer you press down towards the thumb joint, the firmer it gets, just as steak firms up as it cooks. When it's done to your liking, set aside on a warm plate to rest before serving.

GIN, SWEAT AND TEARS

The Perfect Baked Potato

SERVES 2–4
(DEPENDING ON WHETHER YOU SPLIT THEM OR NOT)

2 baking potatoes, or the number   **sea salt**
   you desire

Before we begin, let's talk turkey about your potatoes. You want a variety with a floury texture to absorb all the butter or sour cream in which the potatoes are destined to be smothered. If I'm in Britain, I'll plump for King Edwards or a Desiree at a pinch. In the States, I'll choose a Russet. In Thailand, it's too darned hot for a baked potato, and I'd probably be thinking about ordering from a favourite local food stall rather than cooking. So there.

Preheat the oven to 220°C (425°F), Gas Mark 7.

Dash the potatoes under a running tap, shaking off any excess, then roll them in sea salt. Put them into the oven, straight on the shelf, and bake for about an hour, depending on their size. (If baking more than one, try to make sure all your potatoes are roughly the same size so they're ready at the same time. It's just common sense, really, but you'd be staggered by the number of times people forget. Including me.)

Serve whole to keep the heat in, with cold unsalted butter or sour cream. Serve some finely chopped chives on the side if you like.

The Perfect Creamed Spinach

SERVES 4

450g (1lb) spinach

1 tablespoon olive oil

1–2 garlic cloves, finely chopped

25g (1oz) butter

1 tablespoon flour

65ml (2½fl oz) milk (I use semi-skimmed/2% milk fat)

65ml (2½fl oz) chicken stock

a grating of fresh nutmeg

sea salt and freshly ground black pepper

In fiercely boiling water, blanch the spinach for 30 seconds, then drain and refresh at once in cold water. Drain the spinach thoroughly and squeeze all the water from it. Then chop it finely. You can do this ahead of time.

In a heavy-based frying pan, heat the oil and gently fry the garlic until just golden. Now add the butter to the pan and, when it foams, add the flour. Cook it into a light roux, then add the milk and chicken stock and whisk into a sauce. The process is just like making a béchamel, but not as thick. Add the spinach to the sauce and stir it in. Season with salt, pepper and nutmeg, and serve promptly.

The Perfect Martini

A lot has been written on the subject of the martini. All of it opinionated. Some of it by me. Suffice to say that a well-made martini fulfils all Aristotle's requirements for perfection, and then some.

The real joy of the Musso's martini lies not just in the skill of the bartenders *or* in the ambience *or* in the history (I'm sure there's still a molecule of Bogart's cigarette ash lurking in that carpet somewhere). It's in the little sidecar of seconds served on ice in a small glass carafe beside your glass for a generous single serving that will stay cold throughout.

SERVES 2

a dash of Noilly Prat vermouth

160ml (5½fl oz) of the gin of your choice (as long as it's Beefeater), or vodka if that's your thing

good olives or a twist of lemon, to garnish

Fill a stirring glass or shaker with ice. Add the liquids and stir or shake (your choice) until it's as cold as the nose of an Arctic fox. Leave to stand for as long as it takes to spear your olives or cut your twists, then strain into your favourite cocktail glasses and garnish.

Drink cold, while it's still laughing at you.

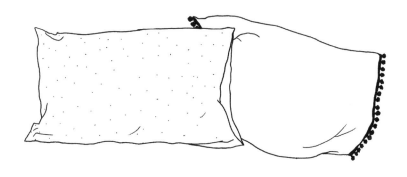

ADVENTURES OF A TERRIBLY GREEDY GIRL

The Cool Side of the Pillow

There's a scientific reason, so they tell me, for why we turn our pillows in the night. It is to do with cooling our brains. Much as I love this idea, for me it serves as a metaphor.

I am a very "active" sleeper. I run marathons at night, and the sheets always end up tangled round me like a serpent as, unconsciously, I fight for the right squishiness of pillow, to move the cat, to maintain a good temperature. If it's not right, I try again. My resting mind is telling me: why settle for a warm, lumpy pillow?

As I wrote at the beginning, mine has been a life lived entirely unplanned. But if I were to see one constant thread within it, it is that I have never been able to settle for something that didn't feel right. If it was ever in my power to change a bad situation, I tried to do so. If my job no longer satisfied, I went looking for a new one. If there was a chance for an adventure, I took it. In each case, I turned over the pillow.

Life changes us. What we wanted when we were young is not necessarily the same thing we want now. My three-year-old self wanted to be a nurse; I gave pretend injections to everyone. My teenage self yearned to be an actress. In my early twenties, I had a burning dream to be a singer. None of those things really panned out. But all those former mes are still a part of the me I have grown to be. A woman with one husband, one dog, two cats and a bunch of dreams for futures new.

Life keeps keeping on. Which means that the pillow will warm up and will need turning once again. For I can never rest my head too long. And while the pillow is cooler now than perhaps it's ever been, I am a 52-year-old woman. And I still don't know what I want to be when I grow up.

Index of recipes

About Kay

Kay Plunkett-Hogge is an acclaimed food and drinks writer, and the author of *Make Mine A Martini* (Mitchell Beazley, 2014), *Heat: Cooking With Chillies* (Quercus, 2016) and *A Sherry And A Little Plate Of Tapas* (Mitchell Beazley, 2016).

In addition to writing her own books, Kay has co-authored a further six cookbooks, working with the award-winning chef Bryn Williams on his two books *Bryn's Kitchen* and *For The Love Of Veg*, Academy Award-nominated actor Stanley Tucci on his second cookbook *The Tucci Table*, and with the American pizza guru Chris Bianco. She also co-wrote *Leon: Family and Friends* with John Vincent and *Cook Yourself Thin: Quick and Easy*.

Born and brought up in Bangkok, Kay spent her childhood between two kitchens — inside for Western food, outside for Thai — before forging an international career in the film and fashion industries. It is an experience that has given her an in-depth knowledge of cuisines from all over the world.

Kay began her food career when she set up a bespoke location catering service for fashion shoots. Since then, and in addition to her writing, she has worked as a food consultant for a variety of restaurants and bars, including the Leon chain, The Formosa Café, Isola del Sole- and The Luang Prabang Motorcycle Club.

Her acclaimed book, *Make Mine A Martini,* was the *Financial Times*'s pick for drinks book of the year and led to her induction into the Gin Guild (in the words of Heston Blumenthal: "She shakes a damn fine cocktail.") and her writing regularly on cocktails for the *Daily Telegraph* and *Sainsbury's Magazine*. She has also written for the *FT Weekend*, *Delicious* and *Olive,* and has published recipes in *The Times*, *Hello* and Borough Market's *Market Life* magazine.

She lives in London with her husband, two cats and a dog.

Acknowledgements

A lot of people think that writing a book is a solitary endeavor. It's not. And so there are many people to thank for their help and support. So (in no particular order) thank you to Caroline Brown, the wonder woman of publicity (complete with golden lasso for tying down the media) for insisting that I write this next and to sales guru Kevin Hawkins for agreeing. To Alison Starling for taking the punt, and to Denise 'The Governess' Bates for agreeing with her, too.

To Team Greedy Girl — the fabulous Juliette Norsworthy, who always manages to make you feel that yours is the only book she's working on even when you know she's actually working on twenty; Alex Stetter, the editortrix with all the tricks; Annie Lee and Caroline Taggart, copy editors extraordinaire; the glorious Amber Badger for her illustrations; Jeremy Tilston for his designing; Allison Gonsalves for production wizziness; Ellen Bashford and Matt Grindon, the Octopii's PR mavens.

Thank you to the folk at A Little Bird for letting me re-use The Art of the Party.

Thank you to Khun Tip and Khun Nai at Chao Lay, and to Khun Jarrett at Soul Food Mahanakorn for recipes.

Thank you for support, inspiration and playing supporting roles somewhere in these pages to Fred, my family, Felicity Blunt, Tam and Bo-That, Vatcharin Bhumichitr, Karen Diamond, Jo and Dick and April, Laura Lightbody, Rosa Sarli, Fran Palumbo, Vince Jung and Jennifer Stewart, Brooklyn Lou, Frank Forbes, Jan Holt, Manny Aguirre for the martinis and Desmond Payne for the gin.

And, finally, thank you Mum and Dad, Lune and Yoon, and Joan. There's not a day that passes when I don't think of each of you.